"*All Roads Lead to Manyberries* is like a script torn right out of Coronation Street, except it's Canadian and it all happens in a little place called The Just One More Saloon in the Prairie town of Manyberries, Alberta. It's a chair-dragging-across-the-saloon-floor earthy read. Ron Wood pokes fun at everyone: federal politicians, 'politically correct' causes, and the national media."
~ Kate Malloy, *The Hill Times*

Praise for Manyberries:

Ron Wood's previous book, *And God Created Manyberries*, was shortlisted for the Stephen Leacock Memorial Medal for Humour, and received words of praise from critics and readers across Canada:

"*And God Created Manyberries* is ribald, raucous and readable [with] belly laughs in every chapter. Ron and the good ol' boys from the Ranchmen's show the rest of Canada that it's OK to laugh at yourself."
~ Pat MacAdam, Ottawa *Sun*/Canoe

"This is a must read for those who have a penchant for political Ottawa."
~ Larry O'Brien, Mayor of Ottawa

"I thoroughly enjoyed your wonderful book *And God Created Manyberries*. I hope you write more."
~ The Hon. Peter Milliken, Speaker, House of Commons

"A lively, satiric take on just about everything Canadians hold dear … the cast of characters is instantly recognizable."
~ Ruth Myles, Calgary *Herald*

"Part satire, part political commentary, part social observation, it has been compared with Stuart McLean's popular *Vinyl Cafe* series, but it's edgier than that … It's a rip-roaring good read."
~ Lorne Gunter, Edmonton *Journal*

"For anyone who likes barroom banter, as well as anyone who wants to trump friends over who knows what about the political scene and media, Ron Wood's *And God Created Manyberries* is a must read. In a nutshell, the book resembles *Corner Gas* meets *Cheers* meets *The Daily Show*. ... *And God Created Manyberries* subtly and humorously reminds the reader that any government cannot function efficiently without the active participation of its citizens."
~ Owais Siddiqui, *Encore*

"Absolutely loved the book. Felt like a regular at the Ranchmen's at the end of it. Loved the characters – reminded me of Spike Milligan's *Puckoon*, an hilarious tale about a fictional village in Ireland."
~ Sean Durkin, *Embassy*

"The [characters] are so life-like one ... could almost name them."
~ Delynda Pilon, *40 Mile County Commentator/Courier*

"The small-town folks in Calgarian's humorous book are universally Canadian."
~ Dave Sulz, *Lethbridge Herald*

"He simply invites readers to pull up a chair, and listen in."
~ Dave Brown, *Ottawa Citizen*

All Roads Lead to Manyberries

All Roads Lead to Manyberries

Ron Wood

Frontenac House

Book and cover design: Epix Design
Cover image: Vance Rodewalt
Author photo: Michael R. Wood
Editorial assistance: Krista Wiebe

Library and Archives Canada Cataloguing in Publication

Wood, Ron, 1942-
All roads lead to Manyberries / Ron Wood.

ISBN 978-1-897181-41-6

1. Manyberries (Alta.)--Anecdotes. 2. Manyberries (Alta.)--Humor.
3. Canada--Politics and government--2006- --Humor. 4. Canadian wit and humor (English). I. Title.

FC3661.3.W64 2010   971.23'4   C2010-902633-0

We acknowledge the support of the Canada Council for the Arts for our publishing program. We also acknowledge the support of The Alberta Foundation for the Arts.

Alberta Foundation for the Arts

Canada Council for the Arts   Conseil des Arts du Canada

Printed and bound in Canada
Published by Frontenac House Ltd.
1138 Frontenac Avenue S.W.
Calgary, Alberta, T2T 1B6, Canada
Tel: 403-245-2491 Fax: 403-245-2380
editor@frontenachouse.com   www.frontenachouse.com

Contents

Prologue

I am pleased to report that very little has changed in and around Manyberries or at the Southern Ranchmen's Inn or even here in The Just One More Saloon since my last dispatch. The title of that was *And God Created Manyberries,* and since then I have been swamped by several thou … well, some inquiries as to how I happened on that title.

Many years ago as an impressionable youth I saw the first movie that starred Brigitte Bardot, which made her an international star and the subject of countless male fantasies. The title was "And God Created Woman". The opening scene had Brigitte lying nude and facedown on a draped pedestal. For younger readers, this was before she started saving seals.

Bardot's debut created such a lasting impression that I have often thought of writing to Katie Couric to suggest that she re-create the scene while the opening credits roll for the CBS News program she anchors. There is no doubt in my mind that this would attract a whole new generation of viewers who rely on Twitter for their essential in-depth information. There are millions of these Twitteriots out there and all the major television networks are frantically searching for ways to add them to their audiences. It would be my plan, if it works for Katie, to draw it to the attention of Peter Mansbridge and then Lloyd Robertson if he hasn't retired, and if it works for them, suggest it to Kevin Newman. After that, there's a franchise opportunity here for sales to local news anchors.

Trying to top *And God Created Manyberries* as a book title was a major challenge and many hours were spent in research and discussion until we finally stumbled on *All Roads Lead to Manyberries*, even if it isn't exactly true. "God's Still Workin' on Manyberries" as a title was rejected out of hand because it was felt that there is no need for any further work on Manyberries by God or anyone else because not even God can improve on His or Her perfection. The author, having spent a lot of time in Ottawa, does not wish to offend anyone, especially those who want to rewrite the National Anthem, or those who don't, so the His or Her designation leaves the choice to the reader.

Another argument erupted when somebody stated that God did not make a mistake when He/She created Manyberries because God is infallible. My own counter-argument was that if there were any truth to one of the greatest songs ever written and recorded, God *was* fallible. The song title was "It Wasn't God Who Made Honky Tonk Angels" and it is my long-held opinion that if God didn't make all the Honky Tonk Angels I've met over the years it *was* a mistake or an oversight of Biblical proportions. But I am grateful for their existence no matter who takes credit for their creation.

As for the roads, there are only three that lead, indirectly, to Manyberries. The one from the west stops abruptly at the one that runs northish and southish over on the east side of the hamlet. Our forefathers and foremothers apparently decided there was no need for a road leading to Manyberries from the east. Their descendants sometimes agree with that early decision, especially during federal elections when some federal political leaders are out scouring the countryside looking for votes in remote corners of Canada.

There are some old and musty academics who will argue that All Roads Lead only to either Kashgar or Rome, but we disagree. We will concede when all roads did lead to those two places they were undoubtedly better maintained than the ones we travel on around here. And we don't have vineyards like they probably have up and down the Appian Way, nor do any caravans loaded with silk pass by this way. Some members of the historic Northwest Mounted Police no doubt wore silk undergarments but they were recruited from faraway places like England. Around Manyberries anybody who owned a silk garment would wear it on the outside as a sign of rank in the community. Old Rutherford sometimes dons a silk cravat and local opinion overwhelmingly sees that as about as rank as anybody could ever get.

Another title we pondered was *Zhuangzi*, in deference to a 2500-year-old Chinese classic, but we rejected this on several grounds. One was plagiarism, although, realistically, after two and one-half millennia there really isn't much likelihood that the author's estate would press charges too forcefully. A more telling concern was that the original version of *Zhuangzi* spent a lot of time on the subject of talking trees. We don't have many trees of any kind around Manyberries, let alone the talking kind, although just about everybody in town knows how to butcher the deer he or she shoots. Those were two important elements in that ancient tome: talking trees and philosophical butchers. Every individual in Manyberries is a philosopher and on many nights, except Sundays when The Just One More Saloon isn't open, you can often see regular patrons of the establishment talking to shrubs as they make their way home. There is really no need for talking trees when you are blessed with listening shrubs. No ancient Chinese philosopher/author is likely to challenge that.

It has been said that Manyberries is the home of some of the most sagacious political observers you'll find anywhere nowadays. I won't argue with that but nobody here has ever said anything about visiting northern Michigan. They were also called perspicacious and I can't argue with that because I have no idea where in the world that is, although it looks like it could be Greek.

But it can be argued that our little hamlet is the Athens of the prairies, and The Just One More the equivalent of the Agora. In Athens, political issues of the day were debated by the Sophists, and the difference here is we sit on chairs to do our talking across and around a table which is kept loaded with high-energy beverages to sustain the debates long into the evenings and sometimes beyond, into the nights.

The most regular regulars who gather daily except Sundays to mull the great issues of the day will be familiar to readers of *And God Created Manyberries*. Perley still makes his rounds as our postal delivery person and sorts the mail as our postal clerk. He still gets no money for doing this or recognition or consent from Ottawa because we don't think it is any of Ottawa's business how we go about getting our mail. His reward for this unflagging volunteer activity is invitations at every home in Manyberries to drop in from time to time for a little refreshment.

Purvis continues to serve as our retired rancher. He retired at the urging of his wife, who wanted to move to some place where there are bright lights and a whirlwind social life. It is a complete mystery why they chose Manyberries.

Big Tim Little moved to Manyberries with the full support of his wife to get as far away from Calgary as possible but remain within a comfortable drive so they can visit their children and grandchildren. If this were Athens, Tim would be our counterpart to Socrates, except that Tim knows the difference between a poplar tree and a hemlock. Like me, Tim grew up in Calgary, although I did it a few years before he did, and we both have fond memories of Calgary as we knew it then. That was when your horses were pastured within an easy bicycle ride from home and you could ride for miles and kilometres over pasture that is now all suburban sprawl. Tim and his wife began thinking about moving when impatience on the road began turning to rage.

Four-eyed Tom remains a mystery and we're unclear as to who consented to his even being on the planet, but he brings a unique perspective to our discussions and debates. Tom rarely ever joins our conversations and spends most of his time working on crossword puzzle books he buys in stacks when he's in Medicine Hat.

Since my last dispatch our dearly beloved Harry Charles went on to happier hunting grounds. We grieved his passing but were pleased when Tim took over editing the Bald Prairie Rattlers Fishing and Hunting Association newsletter. That would be the BPRFHA Bald Prairie Tattler, which is published on a sporadic regular basis over the course of most years, when our stationery budget permits.

Old Rutherford and the Mrs are still with us, still spending the warm months tanning naked as jaybirds and winter months operating and using the tanning parlour they set up in an old trailer they have in their backyard. We think that individually they have surpassed Methuselah and together any other historic figure, Biblical or otherwise, who lived from antiquity forward.

Our anchor is Hazel, who operates The Just One More Saloon and without whom we would be lost and wandering among the forlorn. Politically, Hazel, I think, is a libertarian anarchist. Physically she is the embodiment of all womankind and intellectually so far ahead of those of us who gather daily to worship her there is no known means of measuring the distance. To be honest we also worship that which Hazel serves us on a daily basis, except Sundays when she claims her mental health demands some respite from six consecutive days of blithering insanity, which is us.

As for myself, when I first arrived in Manyberries after an all-too-long sojourn in Ottawa, I just kept wandering with my cell phone and brief case until I ran into somebody who asked why I was packing those things around. It was then I knew I'd found a home.

Prior to your own visit to Manyberries you should become acquainted with the strict protocols you will encounter at The Just One More Saloon. The Manyberries Official Cocktail Hour (MOCH) begins at 5 pm sharp. That does not mean you can't arrive earlier, noon for instance, as some of us do, if you bring something to the debate. The rule is whoever arrives first has choice of first topic for discussion. On some days MOCH becomes MOOCH, the Manyberries Official Officers Cocktail Hour, because we are all officers of the aforementioned fishing and hunting association. MACH and MACHO are still under discussion as acronyms for the same gathering on other days, but we're struggling with both.

You will not question, mention or even arch an eyebrow when Hazel places various drinking vessels in front of me and from which I drink my wine. She has a vast array of flea market treasures which includes very old jelly, jam, mayonnaise, peanut butter jars and other containers with labels she has collected over the years and which, nearly every day without comment, she puts in front of me to accompany the carafes. Nobody has ever asked because they know Hazel won't tell, and I don't know.

I was informed that every book that has more than a few chapters must have a prologue, so this has been it. I don't know what I'll do when I get to the end and have to write a Conlogue.

Big Tim Little Comes to Town

I was sitting over in a dark corner reading, trying to stay focused enough to comprehend *The Name of the Rose* by Umberto Eco. I had purchased a clip-on reading light on a recent trip to Medicine Hat and was giving it a test run. The way I had it figured, it would come in handy on those days when I felt like retiring to the Manyberries Library at noon to wait for the cocktail hour to begin. Actually Manyberries doesn't have a library per se so the Ranchmen's performs that function in addition to its more conventional role, and it's certainly convenient because I don't have far to walk from the library to the saloon. I was on page 10 for the third time when Perley approached.

"Have you met Timothy Little?" he asked, "because if you haven't, you should join us at the table. He's the guy who bought that lot from Old Rutherford and built a house. He moved down from Calgary to retire."

I looked over at our usual table and was surprised to see Purvis and Four-eyed Tom sitting there with a man who looked like he could crush beer barrels between his fingers and wrestle grizzly bears with his free hand. Sitting down he looked taller than me standing up. I looked at my watch and realized the cocktail hour had commenced without my noticing. I picked up my carafe and stemware, which that day was an old-fashioned beer glass, and ambled over to our regular table where Perley made the introductions. Timothy Little stood and extended a hand big enough to play "what am I holding" with a soccer ball.

"Mr. Little," I said, "welcome to Manyberries. We knew you were in town but figured you'd need some time to settle in before we dropped by to officially welcome you."

"Name's Timothy," he said, "but my friends call me Tim for short."

Four-eyed Tom laughed and said, "Do you get it, Tim for short, from a guy his size?"

"I think so, Tom, if that's what he intended. Those crossword puzzles are obviously working for you."

"What are you reading?" Tim asked me.

"It's *The Name of the Rose*," I said.

"Ah yes, by Eco, great book. Thing has been translated into just about every civilized language. I'd bet a lot of people don't get much beyond page 10," Tim said. "How far along are you?"

"Oh, I just started it, but I'm up to page 100," I lied.

"Mostly he reads hunting and fishing magazines," Purvis told Tim, "and old copies of Playboy. Claims he's looking for photos of old girlfriends."

"The fellas here tell me they all love to hunt and fish, so we have a lot in common, but you're the only one who plays golf." Tim said.

"If you can call what I do golfing, yep, for once they're telling the truth."

"We should get out and play a few rounds," Tim suggested. "I love the game, but I'll tell you up front, at my age I can't drive a ball much beyond 300 yards."

"Nor me," I said and this time I wasn't lying. In fact if I'd said that 20 years earlier I still wouldn't have been lying.

"Big Tim has agreed to take on the publishing and editing of the Bald Prairie Tattler," Purvis told me, "and we've invited him to join the Bald Prairie Rattlers Hunting and Fishing Club."

"That's great," I said, "welcome to the club and to your new responsibilities. Getting the Tattler out in timely fashion has been a challenge since we lost our editor emeritus."

"If you guys agree, I was thinking my first editorial would be self-introductory. I'll explain how we decided to leave Calgary and settle here because this place still has a heart and soul. I might spice it up a bit with a rant about stupid Albertans who don't vote."

"If you say something bad about Calgary you'll have to write something worse about Toronto," Four-eyed Tom told him. "You know, for balance."

He got nods of agreement from around the table. "Every issue," Perley said, "will have to have something about stupid politicians too, or else the readers will wonder if we've gone soft."

"Just remember," Purvis said, "the Tattler supports free enterprise and opposes high taxes and government handouts to special interest groups."

"And that includes farmers and ranchers," Perley added. "Especially farmers and ranchers."

"I didn't say that," Purvis spluttered. "Those aren't handouts. That's assistance in hard times for backbone industries with special needs."

"I understand you're retired," Tim said to me. "What do you do to pass the time?"

"Nothing. I do as little as possible as often as possible. Although I do hit golf balls against a canvas tarp in my backyard and practise fly-casting out on the prairie. And I have an old worn-out carpet where I practise putting."

"And he writes letters to editors that he never sends," Perley interrupted. "But he does send the letters he writes to the government in Edmonton asking for grant money so we can build a golf course here."

"I also brew up rhubarb wine every year and am reading up on European-style soups," I told Tim. "And sometimes the rhubarb wine even has some alcohol content. If it doesn't I soak down my compost pile with it."

"Geez, and here I thought retirement was a time in your life when you could slow down and smell the flowers," Tim said. "I thought *I* was busy, and I'm only semi-retired."

"I read in a Calgary newspaper that life up there is what the writer called frantic," Four-eyed Tom said. "They should come down here to Manyberries if they want to see frantic."

"Tom spends most of his days doing crossword puzzles," Perley explained, "and waiting for his pension cheques."

"I'd better not tell my wife that we left one rat race for another," Tim said, "or she'll want to move to a small town."

"You know, it's too bad we don't have any rats in Alberta. If we had rats we could hold an annual rat race here. That'd put Manyberries on the maps of the world," Purvis said.

"But where'd we find the people who'd have time to organize it?" Four-eyed Tom asked him.

Purvis didn't have an answer.

The Old and the Restless

I have one dark and shameful secret that I've never shared with anybody in Manyberries, not even Hazel. I sometimes watch The Young and the Restless on television before trekking several hundred yards to the Ranchmen's Just One More Saloon for the cocktail hour. On other occasions, if I arrive early and Hazel is watching the show – which she does nearly every day – I pretend to ignore the TV, but surreptitiously I'll be listening to every word. I have a hunch that Nikki and Victor will eventually reunite and I don't want to miss that when it happens.

On this one day, as the last commercial rolled, Hazel came to the table with another carafe. "The plot is getting pretty bizarre," she said. "It's a little too far over the top for me. Katherine is either dead or else she's not dead and it's somebody else in the casket. And that's either her ghost or the ghost of somebody else watching and commenting on the proceedings. It's all too damned weird."

"Did Nikki and Victor get back together?" I asked.

"So you watch The Y and the R?"

"No, no, not at all. I was in line at the Co-op store in The Hat. I saw the front cover of a soap opera magazine and one of the teaser headlines asked if Nikki and Victor remarrying was in the cards."

"Well, if you haven't started watching it, don't. It's addictive as hell. At least it was until they started getting silly. I wonder if all the old gals who've been following it for years are sticking with it."

"I don't know," I said, "but if you'd like I could come in early and we could watch it together and maybe I could help, umm, ah, with fresh eyes, sort out the plot line if it's getting confusing."

"Thanks, but I wouldn't ask a man to watch that. Mainly because I don't know any real man who would."

"True enough. Anyway, I brought you a story I got off Sympatico that I thought would give you a chuckle. It's about a 107-year-old woman in New Brunswick who's never missed voting." I handed the printout to Hazel.

"That's interesting, I had one sort of like this for you," she said. "My story was about a 107-year-old woman in England who never once had sex." Four-eyed Tom was just about to take his usual place but abruptly changed direction and headed for another table over in the dark corner.

"Don't you want to hear why, Tom?" Hazel asked, and he shook his head while she resumed reading my printout.

"This old New Brunswick girl," Hazel continued, reading the printout I had given her, "says they always voted Liberal when her husband was alive, but she changed her mind this time. I hope she switched to the Conservatives so she can brag she helped send Stephen back as Prime Minister."

"What about the old girl who never had sex?" I asked. "Was she a nun?"

"From what I've read, collars never stopped priests so I wouldn't bet that a habit stopped every nun who wore one. No, she was not a nun. She just said that she decided early on that sex wasn't worth all the bother."

"Well, maybe she had a point," I said and immediately regretted my words. Hazel gave me one of her steely-eyed looks and shook her head.

"You know, you can be awfully careless in conversation sometimes."

"Yeah, I know but let me dig myself out a little here. Consider her age – born early in the last century, most of the eligible men killed in World War One, even more of them in Two, and parents who were raised in the Victorian Age. Could be she never even went out on whatever they called a date back then."

My feeble recovery attempt obviously didn't impress her because she just shook her head again and rolled her eyes.

To my relief, Perley, Purvis and Big Tim Little arrived. They were just about to settle down when Hazel informed them "we were just talking about having sex."

They immediately wheeled around as one and headed over to join Four-eyed Tom. "I mean a 107-year-old woman having sex," she explained. They kept on walking.

"Speaking of conversational carelessness," I said. Hazel told me to shut up and drink.

Big Tim Settles In

I had arrived a little early for the cocktail hour, which usually commences at 5:00 pm, and was awaiting the arrival of the rest of the club when Big Tim Little came in and joined me. He said his wife had gone up to Calgary to visit the grandchildren so he'd decided to have one of Hazel's special hamburgers for lunch. I explained I had arrived a little early to return a 1979 Reader's Digest and pick up another copy from that same year. At the door to the stairs leading up to the rooms above, there is an eclectic collection of dog-eared books and a stack of very old Reader's Digests that still make for entertaining reading. You can while away the time waiting for the cocktail hour with an RD and a carafe or two of wine.

"So, you're all settled in and prepared to spend eternity in Manyberries?" I asked. Eternity, for some us, is defined as the period between when we wake up and when Hazel opens the doors here. *Here* is The Just One More Saloon, the beating heart of central Manyberries. For others, eternity might last a little bit longer.

"Yep, can't be any more comfortable than we are now and couldn't have found a better place to settle," he said. "We looked at Onefour but it doesn't have any nightlife." Onefour is not far from Manyberries and is so named because at one time it was 14 miles from somewhere else. It does not boast a saloon.

"You know," I told Tim, "when you bought that lot from Old Rutherford, Perley thought you and your wife had three kids. Were those your grandchildren?"

Tim told me the children accompanying him and his wife that day were indeed their grandchildren and that Perley had made a mistaken assumption. Their children were grown up, married and still working, and couldn't afford to live in Manyberries, what with careers and all.

"Besides, they still like Calgary and can't understand why some of us oldtimers don't. But I have to tell you, my wife was flattered when she heard that Perley thought those were our kids."

Tim and I grew up in Calgary, although my growing-up years came before his, but we both remember when it was a small enough city that you could pasture your horses fairly close to your home. Tim had discovered Manyberries while down here hunting antelope and had been enamoured of the place ever since. His wife had grown up on a ranch in Alberta and could think of no better place to live than in a hamlet surrounded by ranches.

I said Tim was a newcomer but, strictly speaking, that isn't correct. You only have to be in Manyberries for a day or two and you're made as welcome and become as much a fixture as anybody who's lived here a lifetime. That's how friendly our little hamlet is.

Which reminds me of an interview a colleague conducted on CJOH Television when I worked there back in the 1970s. It was a feature on Perth, Ontario, a town of 6,000 or so about 50 miles southwest of Ottawa. An elderly woman who'd lived there all her life was singing the praises of her hometown. The interviewer asked if people found it easy to fit in if they moved to Perth and she said he would have to ask the newcomers across the street because she didn't know and hadn't had time to meet them. He asked her how long the newcomers had been living across the street and she said she thought it was between 10 and 15 years.

Educating Manyberries

"Fellas, I think I've found a way to make our future secure and prosperous," Purvis said, "and it won't take any effort and probably won't cost a whole lot."

"Not more lottery tickets, I hope," Perley said. "We're already laying out 120 dollars a year each and our total winnings over the years come to about 40 bucks."

"No, that's personal security; I'm talking about the future prosperity of Manyberries. But this could put Canada on the world map as a side benefit."

"I thought we'd already concluded there's no way the rest of Canada would agree to eliminate all levels of government," Big Tim Little said. "And if we don't do that, prosperity remains but a speck on a distant horizon."

"Feeling poetic today, Tim?" Hazel asked as she rested the edge of her tray onto the table so she could offload. "A speck on a distant horizon would be a good slogan for Manyberries."

"My grandson got this off his computer mail thing," Purvis said and unfolded a sheet of paper and laid it on the table. "He gets mail on the damn thing."

"It's called e-mail, Purvis," I said and scanned the paper.

> *Now you can buy Bacheelor, Degree, MasteerMBA, PhDD at LOW price!*
>
> *Give us a call for more inquiry*
>
> *No Exams/Interview/Books/tests/classes*
>
> *100% No Pre-School qualification Required!*

*Bacheelor, Degree, MasteerMBA, PhDD available in the
field of Your choice So you can even become a doctor and
receive ALL the Benefits that Comes with it!*

Tim scanned it and asked Purvis what his plan was.

"Well, you know how those guys in Ottawa keep saying that an educated workforce is the way to a prosperous future? I told my grandson that if everybody in Manyberries went out and got a degree from this outfit here, we'd all be in clover."

"I bet these are the same guys who keep trying to sell me Viagra," I said. "The format is about the same, and the spelling and grammar."

"If you become a frequent shopper let me know and I'll close early some night," Hazel said and gave me a nudge.

"Who needs that stuff when you're here to gaze upon in wonder and lust?" I asked, and I think she actually blushed.

"What degree did you have in mind, Purvis?" Tim asked.

"My grandson said with my background as a rancher I should consider animals husbands but I was thinking more along the lines of those guys who talk to people about their problems. A guy could sit here all day and do that and get paid for it."

"So Purvis is thinking 'psychiatrist', or at least I think he is. What about you, Tom?"

Four-eyed Tom looked up from his crossword and seemed to ponder the question. "We don't have any barbers in town. I could cut my own hair and save the trip up to Medicine Hat every year."

"A doctorate in Hairology. Interesting. What about you, Perley?"

"I'd like to be one of those guys who lay out the plans for cities and towns," Perley said. "I'd start with Manyberries and work out from here."

"I think that would be urban planning," Tim said. "Or architecture. We could use a few high rise condos around here to increase our urban density. You should probably lay out reserve land for light rail transit so we don't end up with a mess like they have in Calgary, where they never had a plan and don't plan to ever have a plan."

They all turned to me. "Theology," I said, "a doctorate in theology."

"What the hell's theology?" Purvis wondered.

"Religion," I explained. "I could become a man of the cloth. I think spending my time preparing and delivering sermons would be a pleasant preoccupation, and we can't hunt on Sundays anyway."

"So you'd open up the church nobody attends on Sundays? There'd still be nobody attending," Perley said.

"Yeah, but if he did buy some of that mail order Viagra, some of us might," Hazel said and gave Perley a nudge.

"Well, you spent enough time in politics, so you've already got a background in spreading barnyard broadloom," Tim said. "Who's your role model: Billy Sunday or Billy Graham?"

"I was thinking along the lines of those guys on television who are millionaires," I replied.

"What about you, Tim?" Perley asked. "What degree would you buy?"

"I already have two," Tim said, "but I guess if we're all buying, I'll have something environmental, as long as it doesn't take me 10 years to pay for it like it did the first two."

"So you see," Purvis said, "if everybody in Manyberries gets a degree in something, we can claim to be the most educated hamlet in the world. If the total population all get degrees, we'd be a helluva lot more than that speck on that distant horizon Tim was talking about."

"I might want to get one in plumbing, too," Four-eyed Tom said. "I've never been able to figure out how my septic tank works."

"You should ask the guy who drives the honey truck, Tom," I said, "when he comes back next year."

"Here's the kicker," Purvis said, and leaned in and lowered his voice. "We write to these guys and order all these degrees and then we apply for student loans. Most of them never repay those loans, from what I've heard, and we won't either. If we say it's gonna take us four years to get our degrees, we'd have government money pouring in for the whole four years."

"Well, you're correct in suggesting that this will secure the future prosperity of at least some of the country, Purvis," Tim said, and waved at Hazel to let her know the cornucopias of higher learning needed refilling.

"And at the end of the four years, we declare bankruptcy because there's no market here for our higher learning," Purvis said, "and we'll blame it on the government for not doing enough to keep the highly educated employed."

"Maybe I'd like to be a mechanic, too," Four-eyed Tom said, "so I'd know what I'm doing when I'm working on Perley's Pontiac."

Great Balls of Blowfish!

"Did you read that story about how they're telling tourists in Tokyo that they are not permitted to lick the tuna in the market?" Tim asked.

"Nope, last story I read out of Japan was about people getting sick after eating Blowfish testicles," I said. "And I'm still wondering how big they are, or how many Blowfish have to make the supreme sacrifice to make a meal for one person. And why they're considered a delicacy."

"What in the name of all that's coherent are you guys talking about?" Hazel asked as she carefully placed full containers in the few spaces left between the now empty ones. "Fish testicles? On the same day that Michael Ignatieff says he won't defeat the government by showing up to vote against the budget?"

"There might be something to ponder here about the connection between the Blowfish losing theirs and Mr. Ignatieff's decision to dodge an election," Tim said.

"Anyway, in Japan, Blowfish testicles are way more lethal than cyanide and have to be cooked by chefs who are licensed to serve fugu, which is what they call Blowfish over there. The guy who owns the restaurant where they served the fugu is being questioned by police for possible culinary malfeasance."

"It was the tuna lickers story that caught my eye," Tim said. "The tourists got so rowdy that they had to ban them from the fish mongers' market, especially after one drunk licked the head of a frozen tuna and then patted it lovingly."

"Sounds like a Japanese reality show," Hazel said.

"Nope, the licker was a drunk Brit," Tim said. "For reasons known only to them, the Brits love to visit this historic old place to look at frozen fish and hug them."

"If they're married and travelling alone, it probably reminds them of home," Hazel said. "Both men and women."

It was then that Perley, Purvis and Four-eyed Tom arrived, running late because they had waited in their vehicles to listen to the 5:00 pm news, especially the item about Jack Layton discussing the Liberal decision to support the budget.

"Man, is Layton ever steamed," Perley told us. We already knew that because Tim and I had arrived much earlier and caught it on television before Hazel switched channels to watch The Young and the Restless. I think Victor is warming again to Nikki, although she was back in bed with that other guy before leaving for somewhere.

"Yeah, old Jack was practically frothing about a new coalition between the Liberals and Conservatives," Purvis said, and took one of the mugs from Tim's side of the table. One of the traditions of our Manyberries coalition is you can grab a mug from somebody else on the understanding it will be replaced when Hazel takes your order. When Purvis held up two fingers, Hazel knew that meant he wanted three. "I guess he's still bitter about never ever getting to be in Cabinet."

"Did he call Ignatieff a Blowfish?" I asked. "Or a fugu?"

"What the hell are you talking about?" Purvis asked.

"He's making a joke," Four-eyed Tom said, "about tetrodotoxin, which is what makes Blowfish deadly poisonous and which kills people if they eat improperly cooked Blowfish testicles." Tom then bent over his crossword puzzle book and commenced work. I decided maybe all that time he spends working on crossword puzzles does serve a purpose after all.

"What the hell do fish balls have to do with coalitions and budgets?" Purvis demanded. "Where are we, somewhere over a rainbow?"

"How long have you guys been in here?" Perley asked.

"They've been here longer than necessary," Hazel told him. "So long that they missed the story about the guy caught with pigeons in his pants at an Australian airport."

Both Tim and I were disappointed; a story about a guy with pigeons in his pants, even in Australia, easily trumps poisoned Blowfish testicles and Brits who go around licking frozen tuna.

"You should have seen the photo they ran on Canoe with the story," Hazel said. "They only showed the guy from the knees down, with his tights down around his ankles and packages taped to his legs with the pigeons inside. The guy's legs were hairier than a lowland gorilla's."

"Was he coming or going?" Tim asked.

"Coming. He was arriving from Dubai. And if ever a pair of legs needed a Brazilian wax job he's got them."

I suggested he should have tried smuggling budgerigar birds and Hazel wondered why. I had to explain that in Australia the men call their Speedo swimsuits "budgie smugglers."

When she stopped laughing, Hazel told us she had been surfing the internet for interesting news while watching The Young and the Restless and it was the photo of the hirsute legs that caught her eye. The smuggler also had a pigeon egg wrapped snugly and tucked away in the bottom of his suitcase. She had read the whole story to determine if the legs belonged to an Australian man or woman.

"Wonder what the Australians have against pigeons?" Perley wondered.

"Probably don't want them becoming a plague like rabbits," Four-eyed Tom told him and explained that somebody released rabbits to the wild in Australia many years ago and they bred like rabbits do until they became an environmental threat. Purvis said Canada had a similar experience only it was with Torontonians.

German Wonder Women

"What do you call it when one sex is treated better than the other sex?" Purvis asked. "You know, when they give women something that they won't give men?"

"Access to locker rooms?" I asked innocently. I read somewhere that women sports reporters are doing post-game interviews with male players in locker rooms, but I have never read of any guys who cover golf being allowed into the locker room to interview LPGA players. I am an avid follower of the Ladies Professional Golf Association because I prefer golfing with women, who know that, in the end, it's just a game and don't equate their game with their womanhood. I've found among some men that the balls they drive into the rough, into the water, or out of bounds aren't the only balls in play on a golf course.

Purvis wasn't going to let me distract him with the heavenly visions a male reporter would encounter in an LPGA locker room.

"No, when it's just because of their sex, they get something that men don't."

I wasn't going to let Purvis distract me either. "Well, the women in the LPGA are allowed to wear shorts or short skirts and they have beautifully tanned legs while the men have to wear slacks. And I thank God for the traditions of golf or whatever they call it."

"He means sexual discrimination," Hazel told me. "Because of the new safety equipment German policewomen are wearing."

"Yeah," Purvis said, "they're giving policewomen over there bullet-proof brassieres."

"Wonder Woman wore one of those, didn't she?" Big Tim asked. "Remember that television series, how the actress looked in her outfit? Seemed to me they were made out of steel."

"Could be they'll use Kevlar," I offered. "I think the military folks wear Kevlar helmets, so why not brassieres? They could trim off the brims, strap two together and add a couple of shoulder straps and they're in business."

"I think I still have some of the Wonder Woman comic books at home," Four-eyed Tom said. "I remember she could ward off bullets with her wrist bands."

"I think in the television series, she could have warded off bullets with more than her wrist bands," Hazel said. "Probably could have even torpedoed aircraft carriers."

"Well, you know men have parts that need protecting too and I'm wondering why they're not getting steel bullet-proof things to protect them." Purvis shook his head at the wicked unfairness of it all.

"I think the vests men wear have flaps down there," I said, "although it has been a long time since I watched any crime shows and saw policemen wearing bullet-proof vests, so I can't swear to it."

"Geez, I bet a steel bullet-proof brassiere would be pretty chilly to put on in the morning," Perley said. "Or maybe they warm it up by cupping it in their bare hands like you do with a horse's bit in the winter."

"Well, I'm not saying they should give the men steel bullet-proof things to wear," Purvis said. "It's just that there was no mention in that news story about giving men something to wear to protect their stuff. That's discrimination if you ask me."

Hazel said it can't be discrimination if you prioritize what's important and obviously the Germans know what's important.

Four-eyed Tom told her he couldn't see how Wonder Woman could have torpedoed an aircraft carrier with her wrist bands.

Suffer the Children

"I've just found another good reason, maybe the best one so far, for avoiding television," Big Tim said.

I waved at Hazel to get her attention away from the video game she was playing while she shimmied to the music on her iPod. I was hoping she might shimmy our way with a tray.

"I thought American and Canadian Idol were pretty good reasons," I said. "I'd rather pluck my eyebrows than watch those. But I never miss the fireplace they show on one of the channels over the Christmas season."

"The boomers will go crazy when they find out that parking their kids in front of the television to keep them occupied all day was a bad idea," Tim said. "A new study says television isn't a brain booster like they thought but more like a brain squisher."

"I don't have any kids," Four-eyed Tom said, "and I'm not going to stop watching cowboy movies."

"Did they say anything about watching The Young and the Restless?" Hazel asked.

"No, this is about kids whose parents used television as a baby-sitter for their toddlers. Turns out those kids have shorter attention spans and inferior language development."

"I watch the hunting and fishing shows on the weekend from start to finish," Perley said, "and I pay attention."

Tim explained that the study was about kids under two years of age whose substitute parent was the television and whose human parents thought television was brain food. He said the scientists who did the study concluded those kids grew up with delayed cognitive development.

"Can't say as I'm surprised," I said, "considering that the people who produce all that stuff on television have the same disorder. That Survivor series comes to mind, even though I only ever watched three minutes of one program. I'd only ever *heard* of aversion therapy before that."

"From what I understand, the parents have been buying DVDs for their infants believing that they'll give the kids an edge because they're educational. Wrong. Turns out those kids by age seven can't read as well or remember as much as kids who didn't watch the stuff."

"That would explain why there are so many people who want to be on those reality and survivor shows," I said.

It occurred to me that further study was needed to determine if some sort of cognitively challenged epidemic was threatening civilization. I explained my theory to the members of the Manyberries Amateur Cultural Hour Overview (MACHO) that if you have cognitively challenged people producing programs on which only cognitively challenged people are featured and only cognitively challenged people watch those programs, that has to be classified as epidemic. I think I read somewhere about the dumbing down of North America and wondered if the scientific guys had stumbled across the reason.

Four-eyed Tom looked up from his crossword puzzle and waited for a break in the conversation to pose a question. "Why is it," he asked, "they don't have cute girls doing the weather on television anymore?"

Hazel asked him how much television he had watched as a child and he told her they hadn't invented television where he lived at that time. He added that he was probably almost 30 when he started watching The Mighty Hercules. Hazel said that explained it and shimmied back to the bar for more inventory. There's nobody's sister named Kate anywhere in the world who can shimmy like Hazel.

"I sort of liked Mr. Rogers, too," Four-eyed Tom added.

Loving the Uniform

"You've spent a lot of time in Ontario, right?" Big Tim asked me as I slid into my chair with an enormous sigh of relief. I'd had an extremely busy day for a retired person because it was comb the cat day. Even with my hectic schedule I refuse to undertake less than one chore a day. Hosing down the Suburban inside and out has to be done only once a year at the beginning of each hunting season. Same with my hunting wardrobe, but I do that three weeks before the season so the articles, especially the longjohns, can hang in the backyard to freshen while drying.

"Yeah, I guess I travelled as much around Ontario as just about anybody."

"Did you ever visit Cardinal?"

"Many times, it's a beautiful place. Why?"

Tim slid a newspaper clipping across the table. It was from the National Post and headlined "Former soldier faces eviction for flying Canadian flag at his subsidized home". The article said the soldier had been informed by the housing authority in Cardinal he would be evicted if he didn't remove the flag he had hanging from his balcony. That was because of a rule requiring that all subsidized properties must have a uniform appearance.

"Ahh well," I said, "there goes Ontario again. They've got rules and regulations and bylaws up to their necks."

"But what would possess them to ban the flag?" Tim asked. "This guy's ex-military, probably patriotic as hell and wanting, as he says, to show support for our troops."

Hazel dropped by with my carafe and an actual stemmed glass container that was big enough to float roses in and had actually once served that purpose on somebody's table before it wound up in a Medicine Hat flea market. "What's the topic tonight? The crushing pressures and stress of retirement?" I informed her we were discussing bureaucratic uniformity, otherwise known in some circles as stifling stupidity, or more precisely, stupidity that stifles.

"It's not unique to Cardinal," I said in response to Tim's earlier question before Hazel's most welcome interruption. "It's even worse in Ottawa. Hell, they've got condominium bylaws that limit the weight of dogs, and the bureaucrats who are elected by the residents strictly enforce it. I knew one guy who felt he had to put his dog on a diet for fear he'd get a visit from the association with their weigh scales."

"But a flag? What the hell does a flag have to do with uniformity?"

"It's the bureaucratic mindset. They've had so many layers of bureaucracy for all of Ontario's history that the bureaucrats' philosophy has become the provincial philosophy."

"What's that?"

"That one thing can lead to another."

"You mean if this guy hangs a Maple Leaf from his balcony his neighbour might decide to hang a swastika?"

"You'd make a fine bureaucrat, Tim."

"How about how listening to music, which could lead to dancing, which could lead to people touching each other and God only knows what might happen after that?" Hazel joined the conversation.

"They need you in government somewhere, Hazel," I answered.

"Or if that condo association allowed dogs weighing more than 17 pounds on the premises, the next thing you know somebody would be walking a horse up and down the halls," Tim offered, obviously on a roll.

"How about if you allow discount drinks during Happy Hour, it might lead to people actually drinking?" Hazel is angry over the Stelmach government clampdown on Happy Hours in saloons. It should be added that Hazel never had a Happy Hour and never intended to have one but still resented what she called meddling by elected rubes in Edmonton.

"How about if people put their garbage out in small grocery bags it'll lead to backache complaints from garbage collectors?" I said. "That, by the way, is courtesy of Ottawa City Council. And, forgot to mention, the bags have to be green."

"This is fun," Hazel said. "Depressing as hell to know there are people who actually think like this, but fun."

"Give them an inch and they'll take a mile?" Tim asked.

"Not in Ottawa," I explained, "it'd have to be in metric. And both languages."

"Always plan for unanticipated problems," Hazel said.

"That's as bureaucratic as you can get," I said. "Because then you can take credit for the non-occurrence of the unanticipated problem. Careers have been built on that alone in all levels of government."

"I could be a bureaucrat," Hazel said, "spending whole days thinking about why you shouldn't do anything because something might happen."

"Get your resume ready, Hazel," I said, "because the civil service is aging and retiring and jobs are opening up all over."

Miss Julie's Bed Bugs

"I've got a question that's been worrying me lately," Purvis commented as he groaned himself down into his chair and waved at Hazel. Purvis and I suffer from the same affliction: we can't sit down without pain, even on the chairs in the Ranchmen's. We both have bad backs. We have another affliction which all the regulars share: remembering to get up off those chairs. "How do Prime Ministers and Premiers get rid of Cabinet Ministers who do or say something that gets them into a barrel of pickles?"

"Well, unlike the media people, I don't pretend to know. But legend has it every Prime Minister has a letter of resignation from every Cabinet Minister in the lower right drawer of his desk. Each one of them visits him and signs the letter and watches while he puts it away in the drawer. I guess when the time comes and one of them has to go, the Prime Minister calls them on the telephone." I paused while Hazel put two mugs in front of Purvis and six more in front of the three chairs that Perley, Big Tim Little and Four-eyed Tom would soon be occupying. There are days, probably about six out of seven, when Purvis and I arrive before the official commencement of the cocktail hour. We take a break on the seventh because Hazel doesn't open Sundays.

"So what does he do when the time comes? Pull the letter out of the drawer and send copies around for everybody to read?"

"No, I think he'd give the minister a call and tell him or her first and then make it public. That's not how I'd do it, but I'm pretty certain that's how a Prime Minister would."

"How would you do it?" Purvis wondered. "Just get him on the telephone and tell him he's fired?"

"No, I'd break it to him gently, like the song says."

Hazel sat down on what would soon be Perley's chair. "I've gotta hear this," she said, "in case they ever publish another book like 'If I were Prime Minister' and I'll send in a chapter."

"Well, I'd get the minister on the phone and tell him we're going to play a guessing game. I'd ask him to guess which way I was leaning in my chair. Then I'd ask him to guess what I was doing with my right hand."

"And if it was anybody who knew you, even if you were Prime Minister, he'd probably have only one guess and that would be mine as well," Hazel said.

There are days when the wisest course is to pretend you don't understand or even hear Hazel's interjections, so I decided to remain silent.

"So instead of just telling the guy he's fired," Purvis said, "you'd lead him gently to where you want him. So before the hand comes out of the drawer, he says he's resigning?"

"Yeah, give the guy an out, a way to exit gracefully. Then I'd tell him how sorry I was to lose him but that I could tell by his tone he wasn't going to be dissuaded."

"You know in the old days, on the ranches, the foreman would just go up to a rider he didn't want around anymore and tell him to roll his soogans," Purvis said. "They never actually came right out and told the hand he was fired."

"What the hell were his soogans?" Hazel asked.

"His blankets and the canvas groundsheet he wrapped them in," Purvis explained. "So those old time foremen were sort of like you'd be if you were Prime Minister."

"I suppose, but at least my way the guy doing the firing gets a little fun out of it. Being a Prime Minister, as far as I know, is a pretty big job and that'd sort of lighten things up a little."

"What would you do if the guy guessed wrong about what you were doing with your right hand?" Hazel asked.

"I'd probably estimate how many more glasses of wine I could buy if I stopped tipping him," I told her.

It was at that moment that Perley and Big Tim Little arrived and Hazel stood up to give Perley his chair. I told them our topic so far was how Prime Ministers and Premiers fire Cabinet Ministers.

"That reminds me," Perley said, "do you remember when Maxime Bernier's ex-girlfriend said somebody planted hidden microphones in her apartment?" Perley asked. "The media went crazy over it."

"She said that experts told her there was evidence that somebody had planted bugs in her mattress so they could listen to what was going on in there."

"In her mattress?" Purvis asked.

"No, not in the mattress, in the bedroom," Perley said. "The mattress microphones would pick up whatever was going on in her bedroom."

"Wait a minute, hold on," I said. "She claimed that the bugs were planted in her mattress? They don't plant bugs in mattresses, at least not according to any spy novels I've ever read."

"You don't think that common sense is going to get in the way of the media blowing this up like World War Three, do you?" Big Tim asked me.

"They call it torquing, Tim, when they take a little nothing and give it front page treatment. It helps fill the time or space between stories about Lindsay Lohan and Britney Spears."

"But if they put microphones in the mattress, you'd feel the lumps as soon as you got under the blankets," Purvis said.

"No, these would be tiny little things, the size of a button, with their own transmitter," Tim explained. "But if they were in the mattress, surrounded by all that stuffing, there's no way they'd pick up anything, even squeaking bedsprings. It's a silly story but somebody in the media actually asked the Prime Minister for a comment on that."

"You know," Tim suggested, "we should try to write a song about bed bugs, cabinet ministers and big-hearted women."

"Out of my league," I said and leaned back so Hazel could put a carafe down in front of me.

"What's the word for loud noise that makes you hard of hearing?" she asked, "you know, about noise levels?"

"Do you mean decibel levels?" I asked.

"Yeah, decibel levels, that's the word I was looking for."

"What's your point?" I asked.

"That if they put a microphone in my mattress it couldn't handle the decibel levels," and she gave me a wink and went back to the bar.

A Touch of Hummous

For lack of something more creative, we call them home-baked Saturdays. Those are the odd, very occasional Saturdays when one of us brings something from our own kitchen to the Ranchmen's for the rest of the regulars to sample. I brought the idea to The Just One More Saloon when I returned from Ottawa. We didn't do it at the National Press Club every week back then but often enough that it made Saturday afternoons in Ottawa somewhat less tedious. My Manyberries companions eagerly embraced the suggestion.

Perley once brought trout he had smoked in a contraption he rigged up in his backyard. It was acceptable to those who like sushi but the consensus was it needed another week in the smoker.

Four-eyed Tom brought in sausage one winter Saturday. It was made by the Hutterites but had spent some time in his refrigerator so it qualified as coming from his kitchen. We let Tom have the one with the end gnawed off because we weren't sure if it was he, or his old dog, Arnold, who did the gnawing. It was remarkably good, as are all Hutterite sausages.

Purvis on one occasion brought in lemon tarts his wife had baked, which were a bit sweet to accompany wine and beer but otherwise were pretty good. Another time he brought a potful of long-simmered baked beans, which went better with the beverages served up to us by the estimable Hazel.

Big Tim Little arrived one Saturday with a tray full of quiche tarts topped with a sliver of smoked herring, and those *really* went well with the beer and wine. These were surplus to Tim's needs for a potluck cocktail party he was attending in Calgary the next day. Quiche is not a staple in the Manyberries diet but apparently is in Calgary.

My contribution one Saturday was my own hummous and

triangles of pita bread I had purchased the day before on a trip up to Medicine Hat. I've always believed that when it comes to beer and wine, nothing goes better than hummous and pita. There are others, all four of them, who argue the smoked garlic venison sausage I get done up by a Calgary butcher is superior if I bring in enough so there are take-home leftovers.

I laid out the hummous and pita on an adjacent table and invited my gourmet companions to help themselves. Big Tim Little dove in but Purvis, Perley and Four-eyed Tom held back, eyeing the offerings suspiciously.

"What is it?" Purvis asked. "Looks like baby food."

"It's hummous," I explained, "and pita bread for dipping." I dipped a triangle in a bowl and savoured it to show them it was safe.

"What's hummous?" Purvis asked as Perley and Tom took a hesitant dip and an even more hesitant bite.

"It's ground chickpeas, sesame paste, olive oil, loads of garlic and lemon juice," I said, taking another swipe and bite.

"Chickpeas? You mean you're feeding us hen food? Hell with that, I'll get a bag of salt and vinegar chips from the bar."

"I don't think they feed chickpeas to chickens, Purvis," Tim assured him. "I imagine they're too expensive for that."

Purvis picked up a triangle of pita and examined it closely. "You call this bread? Looks like a limp crust or something." He reluctantly took a swipe of hummous and gave it a hesitant tongue taste. Satisfied he wasn't about to start clucking, he ate the piece and quickly picked up another. "Not bad," he said. "It's some sort of foreign food, right?"

"It's a Middle East diet staple," I said, "but I add my own little twist by putting in lemon zest."

"And a helluva lot more garlic," Tim added. "Almost as much garlic as chickpeas. I'll probably be sleeping in the spare room tonight."

"How'd you get a recipe from the Middle East?" Tom asked. "You got friends over there?"

"No, I asked a guy who runs a Lebanese restaurant in Calgary and he told me the ingredients. Anyway, I threw this together after I read there's great tension between Lebanon and Israel over who invented hummous."

I had read an internet news story about how Lebanese industrialists were planning to sue Israel for manufacturing hummous, which Lebanon claims it invented. I had brought in my hummous to stimulate a discussion on a whole new industrial project for Manyberries. It would appeal to Purvis if it could be established there was a profit in it.

"If the Lebanese take the Israelis to court over who has the right to manufacture and sell hummous, there could be an opening here for somebody to slide in and corner the market," I explained. "Those guys will be so busy in court, they'll neglect their hummous industry."

"You mean we'll make it and steal their customers?" Purvis asked. "Geez, I always thought you didn't have any business sense after all those years in Ottawa. I was wrong. You have the makings of a first rate tycoon."

"How do you make the stuff?" Four-eyed Tom wondered.

"I buy a can or two of chickpeas and put them through the blender and then add the other ingredients and the lemon zest. The Lebanese guy never mentioned lemon zest so that gives us a legal edge."

"Do we grow chickpeas in Alberta?" Purvis asked. "You know, so we wouldn't have to be buying them by the can?"

"I don't know."

"People grow garlic in Alberta, I think." Tom said. "Not that a lot of people eat it."

"Yeah, but nobody grows lemons and olives," Perley said and took another dip.

"I think if you added ground pepper, it'd have a more pleasant bite," Tim said. "I always ask for ground pepper when I order it in Calgary."

We all leaned back to give Hazel room to reload the table. We thanked her profusely and I invited her to sample my wares.

"Not bad," she said, "not quite up to what I had that time in Beirut, but acceptable considering the distance and the creator. I think a big bowl of parsley on the side would have been a good idea for anybody who doesn't want to sleep in the spare room tonight. Maybe even a bale of mint leaves."

We all watched in silent admiration as Hazel sauntered back to the bar.

"I don't have a spare room," Tom said. "Just the one bedroom for me and Arnold because the other one is filled with my tools and hunting stuff. And the cat's litter box is in there too."

"How big is the market for this stuff?" Purvis asked. "I mean, do people all over the world eat it, or just those in the Middle East and guys who visit foreign restaurants in Calgary?"

"Millions and millions," I said. "I bet there's not a country in the world where they don't buy hummous." Tim nodded in agreement.

"Sounds promising," Purvis said. "Millions and millions of customers and the suppliers are all tied up in a court battle. We could shovel out that old barn at the ranch and take our blenders out there and set up a factory."

"Count me out," Tom said. "You guys go ahead and do it and buy me a beer when you make your first million."

"Aw, c'mon Tom," Perley said, "you're not that busy these days.

Hell, it's months before fishing season."

"I *am* busy," Tom argued. "I just got a new crossword puzzle book and besides, I don't have a blender."

Fast Food Fatties

"I can't figure out what's happening out there in the world," Perley said. "Everybody blames everybody else for their problems and nobody ever admits that maybe some of our problems are partly our own fault."

"You've been reading the news out of Ottawa again, Perley?" I asked and waved to get Hazel's attention.

"No, this is out of the U.S. about how television commercials are to blame for kids being fat. No mention at all of the parents, or that maybe the kids themselves are just little porkers who shovel down everything in sight."

Researchers had determined that a ban on such commercials would reduce the number of obese young children by 18 per cent and obese older kids by 14 per cent.

"I don't understand this," I said. "Where would a little kid get the money to send out for a pizza when a commercial comes on? Hell, I've ordered pizza in the city and you can't get a good one for under 20 bucks not including tip."

"Maybe it's the parents who get the pizza for them," Perley replied, shaking his head in disgust. "What kind of parent would drop everything every time a kid sees a commercial and run out with the kid to the nearest pizza joint? Geez, those commercials are on every five minutes. No bloody wonder they're all blubber. It says kids started getting fat back in the 1980s. That would mean about a third of all kids are fat. What does *that* tell you about that generation of mothers and fathers?"

The story also reported that the authors of the study wouldn't go so far as to recommend banning all fast food commercials, saying that some families benefit from learning what restaurants are nearby and what they serve.

"That's just more silliness," I commented. "Why would parents need commercials to learn what restaurants are nearby? Maybe they should run commercials to tell them to get out into the neighbourhood a little more often." We're fortunate in Manyberries in that we have intimate knowledge of the location of all the eating establishments in our community. They're called The Just One More Saloon.

Just then Hazel arrived at our table and set my carafe and a shot glass down precisely on the permanent stain rings that indicate where I like them placed. Sometimes when I spill I use my sleeve as a mop but only when it's the right colour shirt. She noticed me inspecting the miniscule glass with what must have been a somewhat sceptical expression. "Alcohol has empty calories," she told me, "so that glass will slow your consumption. You'll thank me for this some day."

"Perhaps, but it'll be a day beyond any timeline I could ever imagine," I replied.

"Next time you're talking to Stephen Harper, pass along a message for me," she said, ignoring my response.

I don't know what makes Hazel think I have a direct line to Stephen's office, but since it might boost my credit rating at The Just One More, or my rating with her, I decided not to disillusion her. "Be glad to," I replied. "What's the message?"

"Tell him to take a page out of the English Conservative leader's book and read from it in Canada. This guy over there tells it like it is."

"You mean David Cameron? I read somewhere that he's polling numbers well above the Labourites and might win the next election. What did he say that got your vote?"

Hazel handed me a clipping from the National Post, written by an Andrew Porter of the Daily Telegraph and headlined "U.K Tory chief gets politically incorrect." She had underlined a paragraph that stated "Britain risks creating a society where nobody is prepared to tell the truth 'about what is good and bad, right and wrong,' he said during a visit to a deprived area of Glasgow."

"This Cameron guy says everyone talks about people being at risk of obesity but nobody ever talks about people who eat too much or never get any exercise," Hazel informed us. "That's what we need here: people who aren't afraid to tell people to get off their duffs and do something instead of whining and complaining."

"Ah, but Hazel, that offends our long cherished cultural tradition of entitlement and political correctness," I said. "We not only demand to have everything we want, we even insist it's our constitutional right to be protected from someone telling us otherwise. Let no one dare suggest that we can't have it all or anything else that might hurt our feelings."

"Well, that's crap if you ask me," she snorted. "What's wrong or offensive in telling groups of people they're too fat or too lazy? Or that if they don't want to be fat they should eat less and exercise more?"

"I don't know, all I know is years ago in Ottawa some woman in the Press Gallery told me there were certain things you can't say if it might hurt people's feelings. And God knows if you do they'll come down from their mountain and hound you until you apologize."

"What were the certain things you couldn't say?"

"She didn't tell me that. So like everybody else in Ottawa I refrained from saying anything on the off chance it might hurt the feelings of somebody somewhere. Better to err on the side of caution than to face the wrath of the Press Gallery."

"What's the difference between the Press Gallery and the Press Club you used to belong to?"

"Well, the one went bankrupt and closed its doors as a club forever. The other great tragedy is the other one is still operating."

Hazel picked up the tray, shaking her head, perhaps in sorrow, perhaps confusion. "I don't see why politicians, or anybody for that matter, can't say that people have to assume some blame or responsibility for what's wrong in their lives, especially if they're obese, lazy, refuse to work, or whatever. You should write a letter to the newspapers."

"But what," I answered, "if it hurt somebody's feelings or made them feel inadequate, or unloved or, God forbid, disentitled? I couldn't sleep with that on my conscience."

"Go take a shower," she told me. "You've still got too much Ottawa on you."

"Anyway, I no longer feel the urge to go sending letters madly off in all directions to editors. And if I did, they'd never get printed because they've all taken sensitivity training."

"I've never met an editor but I'm not losing any sleep over it."

"You're looking at an ex-editor," I told her. "I hope that doesn't disrupt your sleeping patterns."

"Drop over some night and we'll see," she said and nudged me with her hip. "Why'd you quit?"

"Got fed up arguing with and trying to explain to journalism graduates the difference between there and their. Decided I could find more satisfying work with people who don't know everything."

"Who won the argument?"

"Don't know. There's no way of knowing since I stopped reading their copy."

"Anyway, I think somebody should invite this Cameron guy to come over from England to tour North America and tell people that sometimes they have only themselves to blame for their problems and quit snivelling when they should get out and fix things themselves."

Perley and I nodded our agreement that it was time somebody had the nerve to tell the lazy to get up off their duffs and couches and do something.

"Did you guys walk here today?" Hazel asked. We both shook our heads.

"So you both drove the whole, what, 700 or 800 yards between here and your houses?" We both nodded.

"Maybe we can get this Cameron guy to make Manyberries his first stop," she said.

Uncommon Scents

The whole sorry saga began in the early days of summer. "So what's on the agenda today?" Perley asked as he sat down. "I hope it's not politics because I'm getting tired of that and the hunting season is only a few weeks off."

Purvis and Tom waved at Hazel to let her know they'd appreciate her kind attention and then sat down. "I hope," Purvis said, "that whichever of you guys arrived first didn't decide on politics as our topic."

"Me too," Four-eyed agreed and pulled out his crossword puzzle book.

"But I wouldn't mind talking about all those special interest groups lining up to get money out of the provincial government. Why should they get more money when ranchers are still hurting from the mad cow thing? And now they're talking about drought!"

"Isn't that covered under politics?" Perley asked Purvis. "I mean, giving money to anybody is a political decision, right?"

"Not if you give the money to people who need it, like ranchers," Purvis said, "because that would come under common sense."

"Speaking of common sense," I interrupted, "would any of you guys know how to get rid of skunks if they take up residence under your porch?"

"Shoot them," Tom said, not looking up from his crossword. "Or borrow a neighbour's dog and send him in under there. My old Arnold won't go near them anymore after the last time he chased one." Both Purvis and Perley agreed with Tom's first suggestion but advised that it's better to wait until the skunks were over in the neighbour's yard.

"Why do you ask?" Perley wondered. "Got skunks under your porch?"

"No, a friend of mine called from Calgary and said he had some under his sunroom and he was trying to find some way to get rid of them. He thought there was only one and the exterminator charged him 200 bucks to live trap the thing. Then my friend discovered there was at least one more and had to call him back with another trap for another 200 dollars. The exterminator told him of a woman in another neighbourhood who had 40 skunks living under her porch."

"Holy moley," Purvis said. "Forty times two hundred? That'd be eight thousand bucks!"

"Yeah, my friend says there's no way of knowing how many are under there. The exterminator told him to fill in the hole they dug and if they dig it back out, to give him a call and he'd set another trap."

"Well, you could always suggest that he shoot them when they come out at night."

"I did but Calgary has become civilized. The only shooting allowed inside the city limits is by police when they shoot moose that wander into the city or by organized crime guys fighting drug turf wars."

"I can see now why you moved down here," Perley said. "Who'd want to live in a city where you can't shoot skunks under your back porch?"

"Well, my friend says he feels violated, like he's suffered a home invasion."

"Violated?" Big Tim sputtered. "He feels violated because some skunks are under his porch? And he's a Calgarian?"

"Well, uh, he lives in Calgary. He moved there from Toronto."

"Oh, well that explains it – only a guy from Toronto would come up with that. Does he like to sit around and talk about his *real* feelings a lot?"

"He should put mothballs around their burrow. That stops cats," Four-eyed Tom said, "Or use something else that really stinks."

"Geez, Tom," Purvis said. "You don't really think that a skunk would find anything too smelly to walk in, do you? Mothballs would probably smell like perfume to them."

Hazel arrived with a full tray and asked what the topic was for the evening. Purvis told her skunks.

"All you guys ever do is talk about yourselves," she said. "Why can't you elevate it to something interesting?"

"But it's costing his friend two hundred dollars per skunk for a guy to come in and get rid of them," Purvis replied, nodding in my direction. "Even for a guy in Calgary, two hundred a skunk is a lot of money."

"Well, all I know about skunks is if you move them someplace else, it's gotta be so far away it'll take them a lifetime to walk back. They always come back to their burrows." Hazel offloaded her tray and refilled it with empties. "Not unlike what we witness here every day except Sunday," she said.

"Shoot them", Tom said. "Get a silencer from Soldier of Fortune magazine. Nobody'll ever know."

"They will if you miss and the skunk shoots back," I said.

"Man, two hundred bucks a skunk," Purvis said, with a speculative gleam in his eye. "I'll bet a lot of people up in Calgary have skunks under their porches."

"I'm going to be very busy for the next 12 months, Purvis," Big Tim told him. "I won't have time for commuting to Calgary."

"Count me out," Perley said, "the hunting season is coming."

"I can't leave Arnold alone for more than a few hours because he's starting to have accidents," Four-eyed Tom said.

"I made a pledge that I'd go hunting with Perley," I explained.

"Too bad, because out at the ranch there's a whole bunch of gopher traps my mother used to protect her garden."

"Celine Dion," Big Tim blurted. "That's the answer. Get a bunch of her music and pipe it down into the burrow. They won't stop running until they hit Manitoba."

"Tell your friend to call me," Hazel offered, "and I'll tell him how to get rid of skunks."

"That's very kind of you Hazel," I said. "What will you tell him?"

"I'll tell him to close on Sundays like I do."

Two weeks later, the subject came up again. I was late arriving at The Just One More Saloon, and both Perley and Purvis were looking disapprovingly at their watches to let me know it was 5:18 and I was holding up the day's discussion. Their annoyance softened slightly, however, when I told them I had been detained by a phone call from the guy whose sun porch had been invaded. "My friend up in Calgary says his skunk problem is nearing crisis proportions," I told my discussion mates. "The trappers have taken four away so far, and he knows there's another, maybe a lot more, under there."

"I told you to tell him to shoot them," Four-eyed Tom said. "They're not indigenous to Alberta so nobody would care."

"What the hell is indiginaditch?" Purvis wondered.

"Thing is, I don't blame him for feeling violated because I had a run-in with one of the little buggers when I was up there visiting him. Actually, with two of them, on two different mornings. Or it could have been the same one twice." I thanked Hazel for her unusually prompt response. She in turn asked about my skunk encounters.

I told her that I had wangled an invitation to stay for a few nights at the home of a friend and his wife in Calgary. I wangled it by reminding him I had put him up for five nights when he was here hunting pheasants one autumn. They were very hospitable and very hospitably accepted the half dozen bottles of the most reasonably priced wine I could find at the Calgary Co-op liquor store. My friend offered to steam the labels off the bottles so as not to embarrass me if others came to visit.

I am an early riser and had gone out on their deck at 4:30 am for a cigarette in deference to their no-cigarettes-in-the-house rule. His wife smokes thin scented cigarillos but won't tolerate cigarettes. Anyway, while smoking and pondering the stars I heard a rustling noise over beside their trash bag and took a few steps closer, thinking perhaps a neighbour's cat was sampling the scrapings of poached salmon from our previous night's dinner. It wasn't a cat; it was a damned skunk and the miserable little beast took a run at me and stopped and stamped its feet. And growled. I did a backwards 10 yard dash in record time to the safety of their sunroom, flipped on their yard light and watched the arrogant little bugger head back to the private skunk entrance under the sun porch.

It might not have been so embarrassing if I hadn't been wearing my friend's borrowed green, girly-type robe and a pair of fuzzy pink slippers they keep on hand for guests. Running backwards in a robe several sizes too large in pink fuzzy slippers robs a man of all his dignity and I don't have a helluva lot to begin with.

The next morning, same time, I ventured out cautiously with a small flashlight. This time the foul little alien was in among their potted tomato plants and I didn't pick him up in the beam of the flashlight until I was standing right over him and the tomatoes. He made the same aggressive moves but this time started to turn his back on me. I watched from the window as he casually strolled back to the tomatoes. It occurred to me that one could use a hypodermic needle to inject cyanide or something equally lethal into individual tomatoes but discarded that as unworkable. My friend's wife had said she was serving a fresh tomato and sweet onion salad for dinner that night.

"Anyway," I told Hazel, "that was my encounter, and my friend says he's had a few himself. What really capped it for him, and he's not sleeping in these days, was getting up while it was still dark and seeing *two* of them sniffing around his tomato plants."

"How many so far?" Tim asked.

"Two from the first exterminator and then he found another trapper who charges $175 for the first and $75 for every one thereafter and that guy has taken two. So he's up to $650 plus GST and now there's a fresh new tunnel entrance. My buddy says at the rate this is costing him he might have to start buying my kind of wine and steaming the labels off."

"Well, I don't have a skunk problem," Hazel said, "but if you want to spend the night, I have an over-sized robe and a pair of very old fuzzy pink slippers. I'd go out and buy a skunk just to get a picture of that."

There's No Lonely in Sanctimony

The whole thing – Mr. Ritz's black humour and the attention it continues to receive – is the epitome of the insufferable, sanctimonious orthodoxy which now reigns in the land, and which makes me rue for my country far more than any looming world financial fiasco.
~ Christie Blatchford, Globe and Mail

"Where've you been?" Big Tim Little asked when I sat down and waited for Hazel to notice my presence.

"I was back in Calgary visiting that friend with the skunk problem," I replied."

"Well, I've spent the whole week waiting for you to come in so I could bitch about your friends in the media."

"If I'd known that, I would have stayed for another week," I groaned. "What did they do now?"

"It's what they did to Gerry Ritz and how they set their hair on fire over his lame jokes about listeriosis. I got so disgusted with it all I almost set my own hair on fire."

Hazel had arrived with a carafe and a selection of drinking vessels. One was a regular stemmed wine glass, the other a beer mug and the third a very old Kraft Salad Dressing jar with label attached.

"I wasn't sure how thirsty you'd be after your boycott and figured you probably wouldn't want to be seen drinking straight from the carafe," she said. "And I got this Kraft jar at a flea market. It's gotta be at least 40 or 50 years old. If you don't want to use it I'll put it up on the shelf with the antique chewing and smoking tobacco tins."

"It wasn't a boycott," I replied. "It was a vacation of sorts. If you'd opened up a branch plant in Calgary, I would have been there. I'll use the Kraft jar. It's about the same size as my peanut butter jar at home."

"Anyway," Tim said, "all we got for news for a whole week, including those early morning weekend network shows, was about Gerry Ritz. That's all they talked about. My God, they even had political science guys analyzing it. You'd have thought it was World War Three."

Gerry Ritz, Canada's Agriculture Minister, was the political point man during an outbreak of listeriosis from tainted meat. He had assembled a large group of political staffers and bureaucrats in a national conference call during which he tried to break the tension that must have been overwhelming at that point. He quipped, inadvisably as it turned out, that the almost daily death toll was like "death by a thousand cuts, or should I say cold cuts." Then, when somebody said there had been another death, this time in Prince Edward Island, he said, "Please tell me it's Wayne Easter," who is the Liberal Opposition agriculture critic and represents a constituency in P.E.I. What Ritz didn't know was that some anonymous little bureaucrat was taping the phone call to hand to the media at a time when it would do maximum damage to Ritz and the governing Conservatives.

"So what's to discuss?" I asked Tim. "The shallow talent pool of Canadian political journalism? Their fixation on the trivial versus an informed electorate? Political scientists pandering, and pretending to ponder, for exposure or cash, or both?"

"All of that and more. Did you see CBC when they went full tilt one night last week on this silly and stupid so-called story?"

"No. Well, I saw the first 15 or 20 seconds and went surfing for a cowboy movie when I saw where they were headed."

"Well, I didn't," Tim said. "I sat and watched the whole thing. And I got so mad at the waste of my time I had to put some warm milk in my rum. Geez, it seemed like they spent an hour on it."

"Actually, Tim, they spent five minutes and 10 seconds on it, which is still a huge chunk of time for a so-called *National* newscast on the government-owned network."

"So you did watch it."

"No, I read about it in a Globe and Mail that I picked up in Calgary on Saturday, in Christie Blatchford's column." I dug the clipping out of my shirt pocket and handed it to Tim. He gets his G&M mailed to him and it hadn't arrived yet. Or if it had, Perley hadn't delivered it and wouldn't until he had a chance to read the horoscope section.

The headline on the column read "A bit of private black humour has the sanctimonious seeing red." I had underlined a few paragraphs including one that detailed how much time was given over to the Ritz story on CBC's "The National".

"I figured if it came up as a topic for the cocktail hour, I'd just pass this around as my opinion," I told Tim as he read it.

Tim handed the clipping back and told me to leave it out for Purvis, Perley and Four-eyed Tom to read when they showed up.

"Man, she says exactly what we were thinking. And she really lays it on the line – about all we could come up with was a bunch of sputtering. But this was what we would have said if we hadn't kept interrupting each other and if it hadn't been so late every night we talked about it." He paused and took a swallow and thumped his mug back down.

"It's gotta be revenge, eh?" he said. "Didn't you say that the media would wait until the election to get their revenge on the Conservatives?"

"Yeah, something like that. But it reminds me what some now long forgotten reporter said back in the sixties when it was Pearson versus Diefenbaker. This guy said to his media colleagues something about their having a government to defeat and he was talking about the Diefenbaker government."

"So the media have decided their job is to defeat the Conservatives in this election?"

Tim moved his chair to make room at the table for Perley, Purvis and Four-eyed Tom. "He says," pointing at me, "that those reporters are trying to defeat the Conservatives. So he agrees with what we were saying last week."

"Where've you been?" Perley asked. "Thought maybe you'd gone off to Palm Springs again."

"Perley, this is only September. I told you I was going to Calgary the night before I left."

"I would have remembered if you'd said you were going somewhere interesting or important."

"Man, she sure lays it on the line, doesn't she?" Four-eyed Tom handed the clipping to Purvis. "She says what Ritz said was funny and that's what I thought. Is she in that Press Gallery?"

"No, they wouldn't let her in because she has a sense of humour," I replied, "Besides that'd mean she'd have to live in Ottawa."

"Couldn't be any worse than living in Toronto," Perley said and took the clipping from Purvis.

"I can remember when my old Dad made a joke once at the supper table. Man, if those press people'd heard it they would have lynched him," Purvis said and thanked Hazel for her not really all that prompt service. "His best friend lost his leg when he got caught up in a grain augur at the grain elevator where he was an agent. Everybody around was upset and worried that it would mean the end of old Jack because he mightn't have been able to get around the elevator with only one leg. We talked about it for two or three nights around the supper table and my Dad was really down in the dumps because Jack and he had been friends since they were boys."

Purvis paused for a swallow. "Anyway, that one night when everybody had talked it just about to death, my Dad said he thought in the long run at least old Jack would save half of what he used to spend on overalls." Purvis chuckled. "The whole table went dead quiet and we all looked at Dad, thinking it was the cruellest thing we'd ever heard, until my Ma started laughing. Then Grandpa started laughing and next thing you know we all were. Still one of the best jokes I ever heard."

When he had stopped laughing at Purvis' story, Perley had a suggestion. "We should write to this Miss Christie and ask her if she'd like to come and live in Manyberries."

"Yeah, maybe she'd join us every night at The Just One More to help us figure out what we're thinking," Four-eyed Tom said.

"Yeah, and what the big words mean," Purvis added.

Tooting at Windmills

It was autumn when we first heard the warnings about the dangers of human consumption of meat.

Some group of scientists said eating meat was threatening the atmosphere and contributing to global warming.

Actually, it wasn't the meat eating that was the threat, it was the source of the meat, such as cows, and Purvis was in full flight. He and his sons have shares in what's called a cow-calf operation. They own cows that produce calves that are raised and sold to people who prepare them for the tables of people who eat meat. Purvis sold the ranch to his sons but kept a hand in the business by retaining two cows so nobody could say he was a retired rancher. That meant he could still legitimately engage in serious conversations about how ranchers are under-appreciated and underpaid for their product.

Perley had found the story about how many cows, sheep, goats and horses there are on the planet and their daily production of methane. Some scientist said because of all those farts escaping into the atmosphere, farmers and ranchers were contributing to global warming. He didn't say it was farting farmers who were contributing – it was the animals they were raising to sell that were doing the damage.

Having spent too many years in Ottawa I didn't feel qualified to join the conversation because everybody there eats tofu.

The scientists hadn't yet been able to quantify the total of the methane exhaust from all the world's domestic animals, but they were convinced it was a significant amount.

"They're all easterners who are writing this stuff," Purvis said, "and there's no mention of all the dairy cows those people have down there in Ontario and Quebec. We had a Holstein cow for milk when I was a boy and that old cow farted a helluva lot more than any of the Herefords we had out on the range. And that includes the bulls."

"My old dog Arnold farts a lot," Four-eyed Tom chimed in, "although he wouldn't fart as much as a cow, but there's no mention of dogs. And those easterners have just as many dogs down there as we do out here."

"Well, they do say it will require a few more years of study and calculation to determine how big a contribution cows make," Perley told us. "This is just a warning that we might have to change our menus."

"Meat doesn't make you fart nowhere near as much as cabbage and beans," Purvis said, "so why don't they study people who eat cabbage and beans?"

"You can rest assured that, given time, the Liberals and New Democrats will get around to that, Perley," I told him. "But you just gave me an idea. You know that in poor countries, beans are a protein alternative to meat for a lot of people. The Cattlemen's Association should fund a study on how third world countries pose a greater risk to the atmosphere than developed countries."

I lit a cigarette and Purvis noticed and it gave him an idea. "That's methane in those lighters, isn't it?"

"I have no idea," I said, "I just know they're a lot more convenient than all those old and expensive ones I have at home that use lighter fluid because I just throw these away when they're empty."

"Convenience doesn't matter, it's the methane that counts." Purvis thanked Hazel, who had just put another load of mugs and a carafe on the table. "If we could invent a contraption to harness to a cow's rear end and contain that stuff, we could sell it as heating or lighter fuel. Hell, if there are that many animals in the world that fart, we could be bigger than Shell Oil."

"There's an easier way than that," Four-eyed Tom said. "There are millions and millions of people in those poor countries. Millions and millions more than there are cows. And they're all eating beans. If we got them to switch from beans to meat, I bet that would make the scientists happy."

"Problem there, Tom", Perley said, "is they don't have the money to pay Purvis what he wants for his steers and heifers."

"Well, I'm on pension and I can afford it," Four-eyed said and went back to his crossword puzzle.

"Purvis, back in the days when you ran the cattle on grass only and didn't fatten them up at the end with grain or corn, did the cows fart as much as they do now?" Perley had his own idea, obviously, for a solution.

"Geez, I don't know. If we went out to check them it wasn't for that. We rode out to make sure they were in good shape and there were no strays from the neighbours among them. Why?"

"Well, if they're fattened for market with corn or grain or other supplements, that's what gives them gas. If you raised and fed them on grass only, there'd be no more gas."

"Or, if you fattened them on beans so those poor countries wouldn't have beans to eat and would have to buy meat," Four-eyed jumped back into the conversation, "you'd have millions and millions of people producing less gas. A few million cows up against hundreds of millions of bean-eating humans and it'd be no contest."

"The problem here is with the easterners," I said, "at least the few who aren't on tofu diets, who want their meat riddled with fat, marbled, as they call it, and you don't get that on grass fed beef."

"Damned easterners," Purvis said, "they get you coming and going. First they tell us to stop raising cows and then they tell us to make sure the meat is the way they want it."

Hogging the Trough

"This does it," Perley said and slammed a recent copy of the Calgary Herald down on the table so hard it rocked the empty beer mugs. "Next time I vote, it won't be a joke when I vote for the Green Party."

I should explain that Purvis and Perley have, in several recent elections, voted for parties other than the Conservatives. One will vote for the NDP, the other the Green Party or the Liberals. It leaves the rest of Manyberries wondering who the subversives are when the electoral results are published in the 40 Mile Commentator.

Albertans take their freedom seriously and worry about infiltration by radical political elements. You get one or two people voting for a party other than the provincial Progressive Conservatives and the next thing you know you've got anarchists running down the streets with placards or something. Premier Ed Stelmach alluded to such when he called a Liberal "subversive" for questioning the wisdom of some government policy or another.

We've had a Conservative government in Alberta for so many years that the longest serving MLAs have become mummified. More recent ones are in the early stages of the process.

Purvis had picked up the newspaper to scan it and his eyes appeared to have popped out of their sockets. "Those beady-eyed bandits didn't tell us they were going to give themselves raises so they could go penthouse shopping," he said.

"How're you gonna keep 'em down on the farm after they've seen power," Big Tim Little said and then apologized for his levity.

"It says here Stelmach will get a severance of well over a million when he gets the boot," I read from the Herald, "and his salary went from $159,000 to $213,000. Not bad for a hog farmer, if that's what he farms."

"Not bad for a hog," Purvis was fuming.

"Looks like power has gone to their heads," Tim said. "It's a wonder their skulls haven't burst."

"Wouldn't matter," Perley said, "their brains leaked out years ago."

"I'm gonna have to call my buddy in Vancouver," Tim said, "I told him last night, joking, that we have hog farmers running the province. Next time I'll tell him the farmers disappeared and now their hogs are running the province."

"Stelmach says they have to pay more than any other province in Canada and the House of Commons in Ottawa if they want to attract top quality candidates," I explained.

"Well, that's another idea that didn't work." Big Tim cast a shadow over the table when he raised his paw to signal Hazel that we'd be grateful if she could shift her focus from her iPod to our table.

"It says Stelmach went around recruiting candidates by promising them they'd all be handsomely rewarded because salaries would be jacked up after the election." Purvis thanked Hazel for her kind attention and asked her if she remembered whether Stelmach had mentioned during the campaign that he was going to shower Members of the Legislature with thousand dollar bills. She didn't answer because she was listening to her music.

"Well, I don't remember them saying anything," he grumbled. "But then I can't recall any election in the last 50 years where they told us what they really planned to do if we elected them."

"You should know by now what they're going to do to us. It just can't be spoken of in polite company," Tim said. "Not that there's any polite company within ten feet of this table."

"Well, in a day or two, anybody and everybody who's expressing outrage over this will roll over and go back to sleep," I said, "except for those radical subversives who voted for the Green and NDP candidates in the election. I expect it will take them at least a month to get over it."

"I'm never going to get over this," Perley argued. "In fact I think I'll put off going to heaven so I can vote against those troughers for the next 12 elections."

"Me too," Purvis nodded.

"What if it looks like the New Democrats might win the next election?" I asked.

"Oh well, in times of crisis you have to let bygones be bygones and support the incumbents," Purvis said. "That's what democracy is all about."

Mickey and Minnie Visit Saskatchewan

"Did you see any reports about mice in Saskatchewan?" Purvis asked.

"Nope, can't say as I recall anything about Saskatchewan mice," I replied. "Can't say as I recall anything about anything in Saskatchewan for a long time, for that matter. But coming from Saskatchewan it sounds like a banner headline."

"Big infestation," Purvis said. "Huge invasion by the little buggers. My cousin Arnie called me to tell me about it. He says the exterminators are being run off their feet chasing them down."

"I don't think they chase them down, Purvis," Perley said. "I think they probably lay out traps or poison."

"Figure of speech, Perley," Purvis said. "I meant the exterminators are doing whatever they do to get rid of them. Anyway, I was here first and it's my topic. And the way I see it is that when people do something they don't stop to think about the consequences."

"You mean there are consequences to killing mice?" I asked. "Because if there are, I'd like to know before I start plinking at them with my pellet gun again. Not that I ever hit one but if, I did, I'd like to know what the consequences would be."

"I'm talking about the feral cats in Saskatoon," Purvis explained. "You get rid of the feral cats and the next thing you know you've got a mouse invasion."

"Wouldn't that be a mice invasion?" Four-eyed Tom asked. He's a stickler for that sort of thing. We think it's because of all the time he spends over his crossword puzzle books. "Because one mouse couldn't be an invasion. There'd have to be at least a few."

"And if TLC ever got one, would there be consequences for him?"

I asked. "Not that he'd ever pay attention if one ran under his nose." TLC (The Last Cat) lives at my house and, like most cats, orange ones especially, doesn't actually do anything.

"No, the point is, my point is, if they'd hadn't had a policy of ridding the city of feral cats they wouldn't have had a mouse, uh, a mice, umm, an invasion of mice." Purvis glowered at Four-eyed Tom as a warning that he'd brook no further grammatical invasion of his topic.

"Do you mean the newspapers up there are actually wasting paper and ink reporting that Saskatoon has more mice than usual?" Perley is a guy who refuses to spend any time on trivial matters unless they concern him directly. He'd occupy a whole cocktail hour and probably stay late if a mouse invaded his house.

"Well, if one exterminator says he's getting six calls a day from people who want him to come and get rid of their mice, that's big news," Purvis said. "If there are 100 exterminators in Saskatoon, that's 600 calls a day. That's a lot of mice."

"When my kids were young I made the mistake of reading them a book about a Mousekin who spent a cozy winter in a Halloween pumpkin," I said. "Big mistake. After that I had to live trap any mice that came to visit and put them outside. And I had to put the Halloween pumpkin out on the patio every year in case another Mousekin came along looking for a place to hibernate."

"Boy, you're so far off topic it isn't funny," Purvis said and shook his head. I made my apology by squeaking at Hazel to let her know we would appreciate a graceful cat-like stroll to our table.

"The thing is," Purvis continued, "they got rid of the feral cats and that gave the mice a free ride. That's doing something without considering the consequences. Then they had a warm autumn with a sudden cold snap and that caught the mice unprepared so they all moved into warmer places. On top of that they're building houses out on the prairie where the mice were living. Every action has a reaction," he concluded.

"This still doesn't tell me what consequences I might face if I ever plinked one with the pellet gun," I said and thanked Hazel profusely for taking time out from leaning on the bar like Mae West might have, if Mae West had ever worked at the Ranchmen's.

"So, what's the topic tonight, boys?" Hazel asked. "How those rats up in Edmonton are turning themselves into millionaires with our money?"

"No, we're discussing mice in Saskatoon," Purvis replied. "They've had an invasion over there."

"Same thing happening at our Legislature," she said, "except they're rats with mouse-sized brains. I hope you guys remember in the next election what they gave themselves for raises. We might adopt a house rule that anybody who votes for them after they did that isn't welcome here."

"When I was young, we used to have mouse races," Four-eyed Tom said. "We'd catch field mice and put them in a long box with lathing to make laneways and turn them loose to see whose mouse would reach the other end first. They should do that in Saskatchewan."

"Rats would be better,," Purvis said and started getting excited. "But Tom, you might finally have hit on something that could mean a bright and shinier future for Manyberries. Do you guys know what a rat race is?"

"I'd guess it's an event where rats race, but it's only a guess after what Tom said about racing mice," I said. "But then, you never know with Tom."

"I'm thinking about what life is like in the city. Up in Calgary they say life is a rat race. This is what you call a play on words. We could have the Annual Manyberries Rat Race and use real rats on a rat racetrack."

"Could work," Perley said. "It's the sort of event that would draw people in from all over, just to say they'd been in a place where the locals held rat races."

"Of course you'd have to set up a system so people could bet on their favourite rat, with the organizers taking a percentage off the top." Big Tim Little enjoys watching disasters take shape.

"We could use food dyes to colour the rats so people would know one from another," Purvis said. "And name them after famous people."

"I'll get a list of the Members of the Legislature and we can draw from that," I said. "But I've already got two or three in mind to suggest."

"Man, this could draw them in by the hundreds," Purvis said and waved at Hazel. "A lot of people in Alberta have never seen a rat because of the provincial no-rats law."

"Except in the Legislature," I said. "Oh yeah, and in a Calgary neighbourhood more recently. Except that turned out to be a muskrat and the newcomers had never seen one, or a real rat for that matter."

"There's your problem," Tom said. "How can we have a rat race when they don't allow rats in Alberta?"

"Well, we'll just lower our sights a little," Purvis said. "We'll use mice. If nobody's ever seen a rat, who'll know the difference?"

Where's the Beef?

"Well, the Brits are at it again," Purvis said before I'd even had a chance to semaphore a signal to Hazel of my arrival.

"What, another memorial to Diana? Declared war on Persia? Rounding up the Boers?"

"No, they want us to cut down on meat and booze," he answered. "That's fine for them because all they ever eat is kippers, but what about the rest of us?"

Purvis slid a sheet across to me that was headlined "'Meat must be rationed to four portions a week,' says report on climate change."

It was written by a Juliette Jowit for The Guardian, which I had to assume was the one that used to be in Manchester, and reported that the Food Climate Research Network was advising that people be rationed to four modest portions of meat and a litre of milk to stop climate change. Purvis had underlined several salient paragraphs, one of which said total food consumption should be reduced, including intake of alcohol, sweets and chocolates. It said these had low nutritional value. I could understand Purvis' concern; beer for him and wine for me have so much more beyond mere nutritional value. It's a vital part of our life survival regimen.

"Wait'll Perley sees this," Purvis told me. "He'll go crazy if somebody tells him he can't have his two pounds of fudge every week."

"And it's all about cows again," I sympathized. "Seems to me they're not going to let up until every rancher in Alberta is out of business."

"That too," Purvis snorted. "And it was a lot of those crazy buggers in Britain who put money into ranching back when we opened up the west."

Strictly speaking, Purvis wasn't one of those who opened the west but his grandfather was, and like all true Albertans, what was his grandfather's is now his, including the grudges and the history as if he himself had lived it.

"It says in there that cattle and sheep are four-legged weapons of mass destruction," and he snorted again. "Sheep I'll go along with but cows aren't sheep and cows were here first. And there's no mention in there of llamas and alpacas. I never heard anything about global warming until up around the time the goat ropers started bringing those things in from Africa or South America or wherever the hell they come from."

I told Purvis that I was beginning to have doubts about the world scientific community. It seems nearly ever day some scientist somewhere comes out with a theory about cow flatulence or eructation. There was a time when they studied other stuff that was really interesting, not that I could remember then or even now what that stuff was, though I do seem to recall something years ago about a discovery concerning fruit flies. But now, and it seemed to happen suddenly, the world scientific community is focused solely on farting and burping cows and sheep.

"Thing of it is, these guys always go too far. If they had said cut back on drinking milk I'd go along with them because I only use cream in my coffee. And what about pigs? There's nothing in there about bacon."

"I only eat bacon a few times a year because of my cholesterol," I said and thanked Hazel for the carafe and glass-bottomed pewter beer mug.

"It probably wouldn't hurt either of you guys to add more vegetables to your diet," Hazel told us.

"I eat potatoes and rutabagas and even mashed carrots nearly every night," Purvis informed her. "And you've gotta have beef to make the gravy to go with them. These scientific guys don't say anything about how you're going to have gravy for your meal if you don't have beef."

We decided the answer would be for the Canadian Cattlemen's Association's next delegation to Ottawa to lobby for a Canadian scientific study. The objective of the study would be to pooh-pooh anything scientists in foreign countries were saying about the dangers of gas escaping from cows.

"Did you notice that other recommendation from the scientists about how to shop?" Hazel asked us and we shook our heads no.

"They say consumers should adopt the habits of their grandmothers, like using pressure cookers and walking to the store for their groceries."

"We don't have a grocery store in Manyberries," Purvis said, "we go on up to Medicine Hat for that. How the hell are we going to walk to The Hat for groceries every day? Hell, it's a 45 minute drive when the roads are clear. It'd take four days and by the time you got back the bananas would either have been eaten or gone squishy."

"Maybe instead of going to Ottawa you should ask the scientists to forgive Manyberries if we take a pass on their recommendations," Hazel said. "Now, as for vegetables, do you guys want barbecue flavoured chips or the salt and vinegar kind?

Racialionization

"I wish somebody would tell me what this racial profiling stuff is all about," Purvis told us as we leaned back to allow Hazel the room she needed to cover the table with our various necessities. "And is it the same as racial steroidtyping? That was in the story too."

"What story was that, Purvis?" Big Tim Little asked him.

"It was something I read in a Leader-Post that was lying on the table when I arrived," Purvis replied. The Leader-Post is a newspaper that is published in Regina, a city east of Manyberries. Sometimes people from there leave copies of the Leader-Post on their way through Manyberries. "It was all about that Barack Obama guy who's running for President down south and it was too long to read the whole thing because it was about Americans and not us."

"Well, racial profiling is when people look at a person and draw certain conclusions based on that person's skin colour or country of birth," Big Tim replied. "It's a pretty safe bet that most of those conclusions are dead wrong."

"Like if a guy was born in Scotland you know he's cheap?"

"Yeah, that'd qualify, I guess, but in the States it's more about black people and well, these days, people from the Middle East."

"You mean Arabs?"

"That'd be the way some Americans would think, probably some Canadians too. But even a man who's on the swarthy side would probably look suspicious to those yahoos."

"What's swarthy?"

"That'd be somebody who's got a dark complexion, who doesn't look like a pasty-faced white bred North American."

"Well, I suppose you can't be too careful these days," Purvis said and waved at Hazel to let her know our oasis was running dry. "I mean, from what I read anyway, we've gotta be on the alert for terrorists, especially in Alberta."

"I wouldn't stay up late worrying about terrorists invading Manyberries, Purvis," Tim said.

"Yeah? Well, we're not that far from the States and a whole herd of them could wade the Milk River and next thing you know they'd be renting the rooms upstairs."

"Or they might carry on to Medicine Hat where they could get room service," Tim said.

"Well, I'll tell you, I'd be suspicious if I saw some swarmy character out there on the prairie, headed north on foot. And if he was carrying a Karamazov, I'd be more than suspicious."

"What's a Karamazov?" I asked.

"It's a Russian rifle. It's one of the best things the Russians ever invented except maybe for vodka."

"You're thinking the Brothers Karamazov, Purvis?" Tim asked.

"I don't know but it wouldn't surprise me that it took two Russians to invent a gun that good."

"Anyway, if I saw some swarmy guy carrying a Karamazov and heading up here from Montana, I'd be looking for a phone to call the Mounties."

"I wouldn't," Tim said, "I'd take a closer look to make sure it wasn't Four-eyed Tom coming back from hunting. Although I don't think he'd be carrying a Russian army rifle."

"What if the guy was wearing a turban?"

"I'd still wonder if it was Four-eyed Tom."

"But what if he had a beard?"

"Four-eyed Tom, unless it was the first day of the month when he shaves."

"Riding a camel?"

"I'd wonder if Tom traded in his old flatbed for a new ride. I'd probably be concerned though if it turned out to be some wacko from Montana named Lawrence."

"So what's racial steroidtyping? Same thing?"

"Pretty close," Tim said. "It's when you look at a people of a certain race, sometimes even religion, and say they're all the same."

"Like I said, people who were born in Scotland are cheap," Purvis replied. "My wife's grandfather was born over there and he was the most tight-fisted old bugger I ever met. I learned a lot from him."

Blow Me Kangaroo Down

"Do you know any Australians?" Purvis asked while I was still shifting around to lessen the contact between the chair and the bony parts.

"Guess I've met a few, but don't know of any living here in Manyberries," I replied. "Why, are you planning a vacation?"

"Why the hell would I leave one outback to go and visit another?"

"Thought maybe you were looking for somebody who knows somebody over there who could put you up. What you save on hotel costs would pay for a lot of beer."

"No, I'm going to write a letter to somebody to tell them their scientists are dumber than a sack full of horseshoes and they should all be fired."

"I gather this is the topic for the cocktail hour, the intelligence quotients of Australian scientists?"

"Well, if what they're proposing over there catches on over here, we'll all be raising and eating kangaroos instead of beef. They're proposing that Australians give their cows kangaroo stomachs and some are even saying their ranchers should raise kangaroos for meat because kangaroos don't produce as much greenhouse gas as cows."

"Have to admit it does sound pretty bizarre, even for an Australian scientist, not that I know any." I waved at Perley and Big Tim, who had just entered. Four-eyed Tom was over in his dark corner putting his pencils away and tucking his crossword puzzle into his jacket so we'd have a quorum.

"Anyway, let Tim tell you about the science part of it," Purvis said. "He gave me this clipping from the Toronto Globe and Mail."

I took the clipping and saw that the story had been written December 7, undoubtedly a day that will live in infamy not only in the United States but now in the Purvis household as well. The relevant side was headlined "A leap in air quality?" and the subhead read "Scientists say duplicating eco-friendly kangaroo flatulence in farm animals could help reduce global warming."

"So what do you think, Purvis?" Big Tim asked. "Do you think this is an alternative to sequestration of greenhouse gas?"

"I've read the thing twice and I can't understand how they can claim that animals that are raised outside and have never even seen a greenhouse are to blame for gas that comes out of a greenhouse." Purvis shook his head. "They've spent too much time looking into those microscope things."

I scanned the story, which outlined how scientists want to use a special bacteria found in kangaroo digestive systems in cattle and sheep. It seems kangaroos don't emit methane.

"This is pretty scientific stuff, Tim" I said, and waved the clipping. "Bacteria transplants, greenhouse cows and sheep and kangaroos with their own built-in filters."

"I'm just an engineer," he replied, "but I thought if ranchers could find a way to save millions in feed costs they'd probably want to give this a serious look. What do you think, Purvis, as a still-active herdsman?"

"I left my reading glasses at home and didn't see anything about saving on feed. All I read was the part about convincing people to eat kangaroos."

The article said a very considerable percentage of greenhouse gas emissions in Australia come from cattle and sheep. It stated as well that in New Zealand, where they have more animals, the contribution is close to 50 per cent.

"How do the scientists know that cattle and sheep fart methane and kangaroos don't?" Four-eyed Tom asked.

"When you were young, did you ever hold a match to the seat of your pants when you were passing gas?" Tim asked him.

"No, why would I do that?"

"Well, if you had, you would have discovered you're a source of methane yourself," Tim explained.

"I've never eaten kangaroo in my life," Tom told him. "And I never will. And I'm not going to hold a lighted match under some kangaroo." He spread his crossword puzzle book back on the table and returned to work.

We still had a quorum because Tom's mere physical presence, if not his intellectual participation, satisfied Robert's Rules of Order. In that sense Tom is a lot like Cabinet Ministers who are appointed due to their wisdom in getting elected in regions or provinces where all other candidates for the party were unsuccessful. I'm sure that someday somebody will write that, for politicians with Cabinet ambitions, the easiest way to achieve an appointment is to assassinate your candidate colleagues. They do it in leadership races, the most recent proof found in the American Democratic primary contest that featured Hillary and Bill Clinton for the joint American presidency squared off against their party colleague Barack Obama, who wanted to be president all by himself.

"You know, in New Zealand they actually thought about an emissions levy on every sheep and cow in the country," Perley said. "I was thinking we should write to the NDP and suggest that they adopt that as policy to push in the next election."

"They'd never do that," I said. "It would sink their ship in Ontario and Quebec before it even sailed. Do you know how many dairy cows they have down there?"

"They'd exclude dairy cows for the sake of the children," Tim said. "Even if they've never been near a farm, they must have seen cows at some point in their lives, and asked what they're there for."

"But still, if we could get all those politicians off this carbon tax thing that they say will really hurt Alberta and Saskatchewan, at least we'd get some cheers from everybody out here."

"I think this bacteria transplant thing still has merit," I said. "Instead of putting it in sheep and cows, they could consider it for human use. Look at all the humans on the planet who eat beans as their sole source of protein."

"I'd rather see them promise the scientists as much money as they'd need to develop bacteria that eat politicians," Purvis said as he waved to get Hazel's attention away from a biography on Mae West.

"So what's on the agenda tonight, boys?" she asked when she finally arrived. "Women? Politics? The cruel indifference of Edmonton? The dignity of Danny Williams?" and she snorted at that last one.

"To put it politely, we're discussing the flatulence of sheep," Tim replied.

"Well, if you move away from talking about backbench politicians, call me, I'll be at the bar," she said, and returned to her leaning post.

The "Civilized" Olympics

"Did you read that article about how the Chinese government were able to keep their Olympic Games civilized?" Perley asked as I eased down into my therapy chair. I've discovered that my chair at the Ranchmen's Saloon has therapeutic benefits for a woefully painful back. It seems the longer I sit on it, the less I notice the pain. My own self-prescribed therapy on bad back days is to commence the cocktail hour as soon as Hazel throws open the doors and to conclude it when she insists she has to slam them shut so she can get some sleep.

"No, can't say as I did," I answered. "The only sport I follow is golf, when Paula Creamer and Natalie Gulbis are playing, and I read about fishing and hunting."

"Well, they banned all sorts of behaviour and possession of all sorts of items at the venues, like crossbows and spitting."

"From what I've witnessed, I'd guess that if spitting was an Olympic sport, the old folks would win hands down," I said, and thanked Hazel for assisting in my therapy. The prescriptions she serves ease the burden on our public health care system.

"The government over there also put guns, ammo, daggers, acid and radioactive materials on the banned list too."

"What reminded you of the Beijing Olympic Games?" I asked. "They ended long before Vancouver. Had you planned on attending and then cancelled because you couldn't carry your shotgun with you?"

"No, just seems silly to me they had to tell people to leave their guns and crossbows at home and not spit in public. Anyway, it was Purvis who saw the story in a newspaper that somebody left behind. He said he isn't sure what it proved but it must be something about what's wrong with communism."

"I don't know why Purvis would be upset. He gave up chewing tobacco years ago and I doubt he ever owned a crossbow."

"But way down in the story, it also says people couldn't smoke when they were sitting in the stands. He got the newspaper off the smoking bench outside and that got him thinking that maybe they're leaning toward communism up in Edmonton."

The benches have always been out front of the Ranchmen's, but now that we have a law forbidding smoking in saloons there are ashtrays beside them so smokers can nip out for a butt when they feel the need. Even though he doesn't smoke, Purvis complained that the no-smoking law was another step down the slippery slope to a pit where all personal freedom was but a memory. He didn't quite put it that way but he tried.

"Anyway," Perley continued "that got him started on that seat belt law again. First it was seat belt laws, now no-smoking laws and who knows what they'll do next. He says it's instrumental communism."

"I wish somebody would explain to Purvis," I said, "the difference between instruments and increments."

It was at that point that Purvis walked in, accompanied by Big Tim and Four-eyed Tom. They all waved at Hazel, hoping she could get to our table with a tray before they sat down. It was to no avail because Hazel was bent over an old People Magazine with Tom Cruise and Nicole Kidman on the front cover and was listening to her iPod. Big Tim took a detour and tapped her on the shoulder to let her know the Manyberries Cocktail Hour was now in full swing.

"I told you guys that we've got creeping communism here," Purvis said when he squirmed into his comfort zone. "That bunch up in Edmonton are taking a page right out of Communist China's rules book."

"How so, Purvis?" I asked. "Are they banning spitting?"

"Probably that too," he replied, "but this big long list of how immigrants should behave looks to me like all the proof we need." He hauled out a crumpled clipping from the Calgary Herald that was headlined "Wanted: workers with manners." He handed it to me to give it a scan.

Apparently one of the brighter bulbs in the provincial government decided that anybody moving to Alberta should be apprised of the "social customs" of the province. The first custom listed was that it's customary to say, "Hello, how are you?" It said that people even put out their right hand expecting you to shake it; refusing to shake hands is considered impolite by some Canadians.

"So that's why you didn't greet us and extend your right hand, Purvis? Are you rebelling against the dictates of government?"

"Read the rest," he said, "it gets worse."

Custom number two was to stand 60 to 100 centimetres from the person you're talking to because some Canadians feel uncomfortable if someone they don't know touches them or stands too close. It didn't say anything about this being especially true if you've been eating certain delicacies.

"Perley," I said, "next time you have a cheese and onion sandwich for lunch, bring a tape measure so we can maintain a polite distance."

The article went on, and then on again, and again. Look for signs where smoking is permitted, be on time for appointments with doctors and such. It didn't say anything about *if* you can find a doctor, especially one who's taking new patients. It also said that it's okay in Alberta for men and women and even parents and children to hold hands. But spanking children in stores is frowned on, as is yelling at people and calling them names in public. Some of the other useful tidbits on our social customs included a warning against littering, asking people how much they earn or weigh, and hitting or threatening people.

"Sure a lot to absorb here," I said. "I think if anybody told me I'd have to know all this, I'd have second thoughts about living in Alberta."

A Bridge Too Far

"What the hell did they put in the water since we left Calgary?" Big Tim Little asked as I did my Triple A personality thing of sitting down while simultaneously waving at Hazel. And, I should add, nodding at the other guys who were already seated. If that isn't multi-tasking, we in Manyberries will never know what is.

"Don't know," I replied, "I was up there two weeks ago and sustained myself on other liquids."

"Did you read this nut stuff about them planning to build two pedestrian bridges at a cost of about $50 million?" He handed me a page torn from the Calgary Sun.

"They're thinking about hiring some world famous architect to design two foot bridges to span the Bow River and the cost is around $25 million each."

"I did read something about it when I was there but I thought it was just some flake on City Council pipe dreaming. You know, one of those types on a mission to transform Calgary into the Toronto of the prairies."

There was a pause in our conversation while Perley, Purvis and Four-eyed Tom all began waving frantically to get Hazel's attention. That's not easy these days because she's always wearing her iPod and has a handheld computer thing hooked up to a television set on which she plays games. Perley finally had to walk over and tap her on the shoulder.

"What's this?" Purvis asked, scanning the newspaper clipping. "Today's topic?" He read a bit more. "Fifty million bucks for two foot bridges! Is this a joke?"

"Nope, it's what passes for responsible and cautious governance at Calgary City Hall," Tim replied.

"Fifty million bucks," Four-eyed Tom interjected. "You could buy Manyberries for that kind of money."

"You could buy Manyberries 50 times for that kind of money," Purvis said. "And we could probably throw in Orion, Etzikom and Seven Persons to sweeten the deal, and maybe Onefour too."

Perley had returned from his trek to the bar and picked up the clipping. "Wonder if there's any chance they'll get money from the Provincial and Federal governments to help cover the costs?"

"You know, I never thought of that," Purvis said. "You're probably right; those guys are just as crazy as City Councillors when it comes to throwing money around." He paused and his eyes lit up. "I'm thinking maybe we should think about a bridge for Manyberries."

"From where to where, Purvis?" Tim asked. "You can jump across Manyberries Creek at its widest and walk across it in summer when it runs dry."

"Doesn't matter where. Hell, we could have a pedestrian bridge from that side of the street," and he pointed east, "over to this side so people wouldn't have to watch for traffic when they come to the Ranchmen's."

"Nobody watches for traffic now, Purvis," I said, "either coming or going, because of our rule that anybody headed to or from here has the right of way over everything except horses and cows."

"Yeah, but they wouldn't know about that over in Ottawa or up in Edmonton. Anyway, think big picture. We apply for grants for a bridge on the basis of it being a tourist attraction when it's built and we might be able to get a whole herd of money out of those guys."

"I think it'd be better to build it over the creek," Four-eyed said, "as a connector for people who walk to get to the south side of town."

"There is no south side of town," Perley said, shaking his head. "All that's on that side of the creek is rattlesnakes."

"Yeah, but who'd know that in Ottawa or Edmonton?"

"Besides, nobody around here walks unless it's from their pickup to the front door," Big Tim argued. "Except for me, and that's because my wife says if I can't walk 500 yards from our house for a beer there's no way I'm golfing, fishing or hunting anymore."

"We should tell Calgary to send for Sarah Palin," I suggested. "She put the kibosh on that bridge to nowhere up in Alaska. And she doesn't have a whole lot to do these days."

"Well, let's make sure she doesn't come to Manyberries – all she'd do is put the kibosh on our bridge," Tom said. "Then we'd never have a bridge and there goes all that grant money to build one."

"Probably, but to be fair, she'd also have to kibosh those bridges up in Calgary. Think of how grateful all those Calgarians would be if it was our idea that saved them $50 million."

"I don't care about Calgary," Perley argued. "What counts is how much money we could get for a bridge we don't need but that might drag in the tourists."

"You could probably run for City Council in Calgary, Perley, or even for Mayor. They think the same way." I paused to sip some wine and nodded my approval, not that it would have made any difference to Hazel. "They'll build those bridges and then clear the tracks for tourists from every world capital."

"They'll be flocking there from all over, including Etzikom," Tim said. "There might even be people in Onefour who'll make the trip just to see the bridges of madness county."

"As an added attraction they could put City Councillors and the Mayor on display so people could see the idiots responsible for the bridges." I took another sip and gave an even more vehement nod of approval. Again, Hazel didn't notice.

"I wonder how much the governments would give Calgary if they didn't build the bridges?" Purvis, being a successful retired rancher and investor, always turns the table around to see what it looks like from the other side. I'm not certain what that means or even if he does, but it sounds like good business sense.

"Governments," Purvis continued after he had taken another sip of beer and nodded his approval, "could save a bunch of money if they took that approach. They look at all the letters they get asking for money and then offer the beggars half of what they want if they don't go ahead with their plan. I call it saying yes without saying no and everybody goes home happy."

Four-eyed Tom was not going to be deterred. "You know all the years I've lived here, I've thought the one thing we don't have and that we should have is a bridge. Just about every city I've ever read about or visited, like Medicine Hat and Calgary, has bridges."

"Maybe we should ask for a grant to bring in a river," Perley said. "Then they'd have to give us a bridge."

Pounding the Apology Drums

Perley was looking a little agitated as he settled into his chair. He waved at Hazel and laid a newspaper on the table. It was a fairly recent edition of the Regina Leader-Post. Regina is in Saskatchewan, which is not very far from Manyberries.

"I haven't seen any Saskatchewan licence plates in ages," Purvis said, picking up the paper to give it a scan.

"I got it from a young roughneck who went over there on his days off to visit his girlfriend." Perley explained. "Just imagine, a young guy from Newfoundland working on a drilling rig in Alberta has a girlfriend in Saskatchewan."

"My cousin Arnie sends me clippings from the Star Phoenix from time to time if it's anything bad about the Conservatives," Purvis said.

The Star Phoenix covers the news in Saskatoon, which is also in Saskatchewan. There's another daily in Prince Albert, also in that province but more distant from Manyberries than the other two. From time to time the question raised in conversations at the Ranchmen's is why they need three daily newspapers in a province where nothing ever happens. Purvis has often argued that anything important that happens in Saskatchewan could easily be covered by the Medicine Hat News and that would save a lot of paper which in turn would save a lot of trees. Medicine Hat is within spitting distance of the Alberta-Saskatchewan boundary and they could easily arrange for Greyhound bus delivery of bundles of copies over to our neighbouring province.

"Says here that Albertans are flocking to Saskatchewan where house prices are lower," Purvis said. "Why would anybody want to move there when there are large vacant lots available here?" Purvis has several acres over on the east side that he hopes one day to subdivide. Some say his father acquired the land during the Depression back in the 1930s in exchange for two cows because the landowner was broke and needed milk for his family.

"It's the other story that gets my goat," Perley said, leaning over and pointing at a headline about Ukrainian Canadians demanding redress for the confinement of their ancestors during World War One. "Hell, it seems to me that nearly every week some group or another is demanding money and an apology for the way their relatives were treated in the past."

"I went to school with Trudeau on this apology thing," I said. "He didn't much believe in apologizing either, for the sins of the past. Government sins, that is. I have no idea what he thought of the sins that are fun.

"Yeah, well, after this, if they do get an apology, there won't be any left," Perley grumped. "We've done the Japanese, the Sikhs, the Chinese and now the Ukrainians. Who else could there be?"

"They might want to apologize for clawing back my Old Age Security," Purvis said. "I've never gotten a penny from them through that and, even at my age, I'm still paying income tax."

"I don't think I'd write them a formal complaint if I were you, Purvis," Perley said. "They might want to visit you and give your books and records a thorough going-over to make sure they're not short-changing you."

Purvis paled a little at that suggestion and said it was such a small amount that it wasn't worth the time and trouble it would take.

"Anyway, I think it's time Albertans demanded an apology," Perley said, "for the atrocities committed on us by the Indians."

"Geez, Perley," I said in a cautionary tone, "you might find it safer to go swinging brooms at a hornet nest."

"No, I think we've got a legitimate beef, and history is on our side."

"Perley," I argued, "if there were any 'atrocities' that happened in Canada they were all committed *against* the Indians – for instance, the residential schools. Any massacres or atrocities *by* the Indians, from what I've read, all happened south of the border."

"You know what Stephen should do?" Purvis asked. "He should apologize to anybody and every group that has a complaint and say it happened because in the past misguided Canadians voted Liberals or New Democrats into power."

"I'd want to check my Parliamentary history because there might have been Conservatives in Government when some of that stuff happened," I said. "No politician would want to get hung out to dry for saying something like that."

"Who'd hang them out to dry? You don't think reporters would take the time to bother checking history, do you?"

"Anyway, back to what I was saying," Perley said, "Albertans should demand an apology and financial compensation for the great Cowley wagon train massacre."

Perley waved at Hazel to let her know our wickiup needed a visit.

"Back in 1867, there was a small wagon train on its way to Fort Edmonton," he said. "It was led by a guy named John Hoise and there were 12 men, women and children on board. They were attacked and slaughtered by Blood Indians not far from Cowley, wherever Cowley is. There were no survivors. If that wasn't an atrocity, I don't know what is. We should demand an apology."

"I never, ever, in anything I've read about Alberta's history, came across a story like that," I said.

"Saw it in a newspaper, back around Calgary Stampede time," Perley explained. "First time I'd ever heard about it, too."

"I wonder if there's some sort of monument or plaque there?"

"I don't know. Doesn't matter anyway. Cowley's probably just a dinky place."

"If we could find somebody named Hoise, we could get a finder's fee and *then* we'd be in clover," Purvis said. "He could sue the Blood Nation for millions for the loss of his family and the land they would have owned if they'd made it to Fort Edmonton."

"There's a lawyer over in Saskatchewan who specializes in cases like this," I said, "although from what I've read he's already a multi-jillionaire from a previous case where he worked on behalf of the Indians. Your victim would probably have to sue for the entire worth of Edmonton to get him interested. And I'm not certain Edmonton is worth all that much after Wayne Gretzky moved away."

"We'll just change the story and say the massacre victims were on their way to Calgary," Purvis said. "That way there'd be enough money in it to interest even a lawyer from Regina."

"My second cousin up in Seven Persons went to talk to a Medicine Hat lawyer about suing a neighbour over a road allowance and the lawyer wanted money up front for the hour he spent deciding if he could represent my cousin," Four-eyed Tom told us. He had been concentrating on his crossword puzzle book and I had assumed he wasn't paying attention.

"I'm not going to put money on anything unless it's a sure bet," Perley said. "And this sure isn't a sure bet."

"Well, so, we lower our sights," Purvis mused. "We write to Stephen and ask him, as Prime Minister, to apologize on behalf of the Blood Indians to everybody named Hoise and any Canadians who feel or felt any pain or discomfort over the massacre."

All Roads Lead to Manyberries

Gilligan's Island

"I've just learned something that strikes me as profoundly significant," Big Tim Little said, settling into his chair while reaching for the mug Perley pushed across to him.

"In fact, when this becomes known it will be ranked as one of the top 10 culturally significant discoveries in the history of humankind."

"Well, I'm not big on culture," Four-eyed Tom said. "There was something about ballet on the television a few nights ago and it almost put me to sleep before I got up and switched channels."

"I'm with Tom," Purvis said. "Although the wife and I went up to Calgary one time to see the Ice Capades and I didn't mind that."

"I'm still hoping that one day I can see Anne Murray in person," Perley said. "I'd even go on up to Calgary if she ever put on a concert there."

They all turned and looked at me. It was a struggle but I finally remembered that I watch a lot of hunting and fishing programs if I can get up early enough on weekends. And I never miss Paula Creamer and Natalie Gulbis when they're playing in LPGA events. Like most avid male golf fans I try never to miss the part where they have to retrieve the ball from the cup after they've finished putting.

"I'm talking about anthropological cultural discoveries," Big Tim said. "You know, why ancient humans did what they did and how that affected civilization today."

"Like what John Diefenbaker did when he opened up the north and how Stephen Harper is following his lead?" Perley wondered.

"You're not even close," Tim said. "*This* is about why we behave the way we do now and how our ancestors influenced that. Like, for instance, why we wear clothes."

"I wear them because Hazel wouldn't let me in if I didn't," Tom said, and bent back over his crossword puzzle book.

"Hell, who'd wanna walk through a half mile of wild rose bushes without pants on?" Perly asked. "If I had to do that, I'd give up pheasant hunting."

"Can you imagine a guy having to sit in a saddle all day without his jeans on and nothing between him and the leather?" Purvis shook his head. "You'll never catch me up there like that."

"For which we shall all be eternally grateful, Purvis," Tim told him. "But that's not precisely the point here. This is about whether modesty or necessity influenced ancient civilizations and their wardrobe choices."

"Even if Hazel wouldn't let me in without clothes on," Tom said, "I'd say wearing clothes would be a necessity."

"Especially when it's cold," Perley added. "I put on my long johns on November 1st and they don't come off until April 1st , except on laundry day."

"I keep telling you, Perley," Purvis said, "if you'd get a remote starter installed, your Pontiac would be as cozy as your kitchen. All I do is hit the remote garage opener, then the remote starter, and when the pickup is warm I walk out, get in and drive over here."

Purvis lives no more than 700 strides from the Ranchmen's. Like all cowboys, he won't walk if he can ride and what he rides these days is a diesel-powered, four-wheel-drive, three-quarter-ton pickup that costs as much as a home in the city once did and might again very soon, with natural gas and oil prices plummeting.

"I guess your Pontiac can't have automatic seat warmers installed, but that helps too," he added.

"Anyway," Tim sort of sighed, "this anthropologist guy in Australia has conducted a major research study to determine why people, especially the aboriginals down there, wear clothes. According to the National Post he thinks he's 'discovered a deeply rooted human tendency' as a result of all his research and reading of the stuff early European explorers recorded in their journals and diaries."

"I thought anthropologicals studied things like petrified pregnant turtles," Purvis interrupted. "You know, like the guys who come down and dig around here every summer."

"Two different disciplines," Tim explained. "In a nutshell, according to the Post, this guy says his research shows that 'people – or at least aboriginal Australians – started wearing clothes because it was cold,' so the only conclusion we can draw is we're kin to the aboriginals in Australia."

"Do you mean this guy spent his time trying to find out why we wear clothes, and got paid for it, and then tells us we do it because clothes keep us warm?" Perley shook his head and waved at Hazel to let her know it was time to start planning a saunter over to our table.

"That'd be the other reason I wear clothes," Four-eyed Tom said. "Even if Hazel would let me in if I wasn't wearing them, I wouldn't do it in the winter."

"And there's no way I'd walk out to my pickup, even when it's running and warm," Purvis agreed, "because I'd still have to make it to the garage from the kitchen door. Maybe in July, but not in January."

"Who paid this guy to do this?" Perley asked. "Hell, I bet I could do a study to find out why Canadians wear clothes and maybe make a few bucks next winter."

"He's a professor at the Australian National University, so I guess he either did it on his own time or maybe got a federal grant. The government down there is probably as loose with its money as Ottawa."

"You can get a jump on him if you're interested, Perley. He says the next thing he's going to study is the point of blankets. He says that, strictly speaking, blankets aren't clothes and early peoples used them. He's wondering why."

"Who is this professor, anyway?" Purvis asked. "He sounds like my kind of guy. He's got a gold mine here. The next thing he could study is why we wear boots."

"His name is Ian Gilligan," Tim answered. "Maybe you guys should write to him and offer to conduct similar research in and around Manyberries. You might discover that the Indians who lived around here wore clothes for the same reason the aboriginals did down in Australia."

"You said this guy's name is Gilligan?" Four-eyed Tom asked and Tim nodded.

"And he lives in Australia, right?" Tim nodded again.

"And Australia is an island. So this guy lives on an island and his name is Gilligan? This isn't April Fools Day, Tim," Tom concluded and went back to his crossword puzzle.

Tim hauled a newspaper clipping out of his shirt pocket and spread it on the table. The headline was 'Dress up, it's cold outside'. It was from the National Post and written by a Joseph Brean. "I thought you guys might be sceptical so I brought the proof."

"Next time those anthropolitical guys come down here to dig for pregnant turtles, we should tell them there's an easier way to make a living and give them your newspaper story," Purvis said and thanked Hazel for her kind attention.

The Mediachurning Candidate

All of Manyberries was buzzing over the election of Barack Obama, almost as much as they were about the snowfall that began at approximately the same time the networks declared Obama the winner. Not to trivialize Obama's victory but snow at the beginning of deer season is considered a good omen.

Big Tim Little was already waiting for us when we arrived at The Just One More saloon the day after the election. He had driven from Medicine Hat after flying in from the east coast where he'd spent a week consulting. His wife called his cell phone and told him to stop by the Ranchmen's before going home. We think it's because she has sympathy for anybody who has to fly from wherever on the east coast west through Toronto, on to Calgary and then back southeast to Medicine Hat. It takes nearly as long to do that as it once took to get to Manyberries from Robsart in a covered wagon.

"I watched the networks last night in the airport hotel," Tim told us, "and was really very happy to see history being made. They've put their past behind them and I bet the whole world is as excited as I was."

"Yep, that sure was something." Perley said. "In a way, I guess, it was sort of like being there at the end of a war."

"I never thought that Americans would elect a black man," Purvis said. "Maybe I underestimated them. Maybe they're different these days from what they were."

"I figured if a newcomer like that could be elected President, hell, maybe some day a guy from Manyberries could get elected Prime Minister," Four-eyed Tom told us. "Not that anybody would want to live in Ottawa. But I don't understand why they keep calling him an African-American. The guy was born there so why not just call him an American?"

"Well, African, American, whatever, I just wish the guy all the luck in the world," I said, "because the way the economy's gone south, he'll need it. And the world is a helluva big town for a new sheriff."

"I was wishing I'd been here to watch the coverage with you guys," Tim told us. "You know, instead of calling room service and watching it in a hotel room."

"Well, if you'd been here, you might not have been watching American election coverage," I said. "Because it wasn't on."

"What? Did Hazel lose the satellite?"

"No, that was all working. It's just that a Randolph Scott movie was on one of the movie channels and we watched that." Perley waved at Hazel to let her know we'd appreciate a smidgeon of her attention.

"It was Decision at Sundown, which we'd never seen before," Perley told Tim. "And not one of those guys fired more than six times with his six-shooter before reloading, so it was pretty real."

"And we were discussing the good manners of the Chinese," Purvis said, "because there's another news story about how they're learning to be polite."

"And it was snowing so we were also trying to decide if we should go out and look for tracks this morning," Perley said as he looked up in grateful admiration at Hazel.

Tim sort of sighed and asked about the Chinese learning manners. He hasn't been here for all *that* long so he is still, sometimes, unadjusted to what's really important in Manyberries.

"I pulled a story off the internet that was headlined 'Manners on upswing in Beijing,'" I told him, "and we found that sort of fascinating. It said Chinese researchers spent 3,000 hours observing the public in Beijing and that their good manners shot to an all-time high of 82.68 on the 'civilization index' following a campaign to improve their public behaviour. It said they stopped spitting and cursing in public and even gave strangers directions when asked."

"We figured if a billion people started giving directions and stopped swearing and spitting, it'd be a whole different country," Purvis said. "Probably more like Manyberries."

"Except for the cursing and spitting part," Four-eyed Tom said.

"I wonder if what you felt when they declared Obama the winner was the same as the tingle the Canadian media were feeling." I thanked Hazel for her heroic devotion to her duties. "The children were just as excited over Obama's win as they were about the onslaught of Trudeau back in the recent century."

"Yeah, I read somewhere that a guy named Chris Matthews on some American network said after an Obama speech that he felt a thrill going up his leg and that he doesn't get those too often."

"Maybe what he really meant was that he felt a tinkle," I suggested. "Either way I'd suggest that the media folks in both countries were grateful that they had a ready supply of Depends on hand."

I think our media suffer from Obama-envy," Tim said and shook his head. They're anti-American as hell, but the way they fawn over him makes me feel like I'm being force fed corn syrup."

It's probably been years since any of those reporters felt anything going up their legs," Hazel said. "Unless it was when they were pulling up their support hose."

The Running of the Women

I arrived a little early for the Manyberries Official Cocktail Hour and was alone at the table when Hazel thumped my stemware (an old, very old 5 cent beer glass) and carafe on the table. The Manyberries Official etc. usually commences at, or within minutes of, 5:00 pm, but I had arrived at noon to return another old copy of a Reader's Digest I'd found in the book rack just inside the entrance to the rooms upstairs in the Southern Ranchmen's Inn. I love reading the jokes that were already decades old before being printed in RD in the 1970s. This was also about a week after the Americans elected Barack Obama and so I was desperate for anything to read other than how yet another Canadian thumb-sucking columnist felt on the night of Obama's triumph. I had begun to think that Canadian editors were going to start digging up long-dead columnists to write about how they would have felt about his victory. I could just imagine the conversation:

> **Editorial Page Editor**: *"Charlie, we want you to come back and give us a piece on what Obama's election meant to you."*
>
> **Voice Coming up from Somewhere Below**: *"Well, actually I was thinking if I was going to do a piece on the election, I'd focus on Sarah Palin's legs."*
>
> **Editorial Page Editor**: *"Great idea! We'll take both. Give us Palin's legs for tomorrow and your straight-from-the-heart thing on Obama the next day."*

My daydream of this unrecorded but nevertheless perfectly

plausible conversation was abruptly shattered by a humph and snort from Hazel doing her thumping-of-the-glass-and-carafe-on-the-table thing. "Men, dumbest things on the planet," she sneered.

I'm always very careful when Hazel humphs and snorts because though she's even lovelier when angry, her anger ain't lovely.

"I'm sorry Hazel for what we've done now and sorry for everything we've ever done. What did we do now or what was it we did whenever we did it?"

"You store your brains in your lap," she said. "You only vote for good-looking women." She handed me a printout of a story that came off the CTV website with the headline "Good looks matter most for women in politics: study".

"I've never voted for a woman in my life," I said after I'd scanned the headline, "so that should leave me off your hit list." Realizing I might have just run on to *very* thin ice, I hastened to explain. "Because no women were running for office whenever and wherever I voted."

Hazel's shoulders came down but she still gave me the look that one gives the enemy across no person's land.

"Hazel, why would this bother you? What it says to me is you, you beautiful thing, could run anywhere, even in places they don't have elections, and win."

"If you're trying to soften me up," she said, "it's working. But can you imagine that more men than women would vote for a woman just because she's good looking? Migawd that means all a woman needs is a good pair of legs, a waist, hips and a face that cameras love and she can get elected."

She had underlined a part of the story that said "…the study also found that good looks were almost all that mattered in predicting men's votes for female candidates."

"This is an American study," I said. "It was conducted by some academics in Illinois."

"You haven't learned yet that men are men wherever they are," Hazel told me. "There's no difference between men of any country." She paused and got a kind of faraway look in her eyes. "Although, come to think of it, there are *some* differences, but nothing to do with politics."

The story said participants were shown photos of various political candidates and asked to rate them on competence, attractiveness, approachability and dominance. Male candidates won hands down on competence and dominance. Females won in the attractive and approachability categories.

"The researcher says this is a remnant of evolution," Hazel said with a lovely humph. "In other words, men haven't evolved."

"But they didn't elect Sarah Palin," I said. "And from what I saw on television she could probably have been put in the attractive category."

"That was about Obama and McCain, not Sarah. But she got beauty queen treatment from the media down there until she opened her mouth."

"Yeah, but that's because there are still more men than women in the media."

"What about when Belinda Stronach went for the Conservative leadership? Remember all that crap about how she dressed and who her rock star and political heavyweight friends were?"

"Too many more men than women in the media up here, too," I said.

It was at that point that Four-eyed Tom wandered in and pulled up a chair. "It's too bad that John McCain didn't get elected President down in the States," he said, "because that Sarah Palin is a good lookin' chick and would have been great as Vice President."

I was getting ready to dive under the table when Hazel said, "I rest my case," and asked Tom if he wanted his usual Stone Age petrified beer.

From Lucan to Manyberries

"I just watched a rerun of a documentary on the Black Donnelleys," I said as I settled into my chair, joining Big Tim Little who, contrary to custom, had arrived before me. Some days I leave the house when The Young and the Restless starts at 4:00. Unless of course Victor is up to something particularly nefarious and then I wait long enough to get the gist of what he's doing so I don't lose touch entirely with the program.

"I thought you never watch television," Tim said, "and now you're watching programs you've already watched? You're older than I am but still too young to be giving up on life entirely."

"I don't *watch* television," I said, "I skim it but occasionally do pause if something strikes me as particularly significant. The Lucan massacre qualifies because that's a helluva story."

"What's it all about?" Tim asked as Hazel put some sustenance on the table. I thanked her and said she was looking particularly sparkling. She gave me a knuckle rub on my bald spot and went back to the bar.

"It was a massacre of a whole family in Ontario, near a town called Lucan. They were murdered by men who considered themselves righteous and upstanding citizens." The Donnellys, according to various accounts I'd read, were, from the vigilantes' perspective, terrorists. But there were others who argued the whole ghastly thing was triggered by business disputes and commercial rivalry.

"Funny thing, you know," I said to Tim, "this reminds me of some years ago when I walked in here and Harry Charles was sitting where you are and I told him almost word for word what I just told you, that I had watched this same documentary."

Big Tim took a swallow that would have half filled a trough and asked me to continue.

"Well, on most days back then, like now, I was the first to arrive but this documentary on the Black Donnellys had grabbed my attention and I watched it from beginning to end." I watch the History Channel a lot, hoping some day they'll get around to Manyberries and do research I can borrow, since I've pretty well given up any hope that I'll do it myself, even though I keep promising that I will, one of these days.

"I know about the Black Donnellys," I remember Harry Charles telling me. "That was as big a stain on justice and humanity in Canada as any event in our history."

"Did you watch the documentary?" I asked him back then. "I thought you refused to watch television, especially during the day."

"No, I learned about it from my grandmother, Jane. She was second generation over from Ireland and heard the story from descendants of the Donnellys and other people from Lucan. It wasn't something they talked about when company was around. The Irish back then brought all their grudges and hates when they came here to settle, and invariably passed them on to the next generation."

"So she told you about it?"

"She told me three things. She said the people who killed the Donnellys were savages and should have all been hanged. And she told me that greed, envy and jealousy are what poison the human soul and eventually kill it. And she said that anybody who argues that one religion is better than another religion has gone to a school where the devil teaches."

"Seems to me," Tim interrupted, abruptly jerking me back from my memories of Harry Charles, "that the world could use a helluva lot more grandmas."

"Harry Charles said there are still some around, but not nearly enough and there had been some over the years he'd known, or known about. He told me Martin Luther King came to mind, and he mentioned D'Arcy McGee, a Canadian statesman of Irish descent who forswore insurrection and was murdered because of it. They weren't grandmas, obviously, but they believed much the same way she did – and history knows what happened to them."

"So I guess," Tim said, "the point is the world has decided it doesn't want any more grandmas."

"Yeah, that's about what Harry Charles said. He figured every time the world ran short on grandmas, that's when trouble started. He told me he thought grandma shortages could be linked to historic events. He mentioned World Wars One and Two, the Cold War, racism and bigotry, and now all this jihad stuff."

"You know what you should do?" Tim asked. "Instead of watching television, you should research how many despots, dictators, mass murderers and genocidal maniacs had grandmothers. I could find room for a few paragraphs in the Tattler if you wrote it up."

"Geez, I don't know about that, Tim" I said, "because from what I gather, Victor is planning to sue Nikki and her new husband over something and I don't want to get too far out of the loop on that one."

"I don't know what the hell you're talking about," he said. And waved at Hazel to let her know it was opera intermission time.

liberals Always Laugh L(e)ast

"Did you read this?" Big Tim asked and handed me the Globe and Mail Social Studies column, "A Daily Miscellany of Information" by Michael Kesterton. Tim had red inked a squib titled "Who Laughs More?"

It said that Boston researchers had tested the sense of humour of nearly 300 people to see how they reacted to jokes that ranged from good to bad, conventional to absurd. The test subjects were asked to describe themselves as liberals or conservatives.

The conclusion was that conservatives enjoyed all kinds of humour more than liberals.

"Well, I'm not surprised," I said. "There's nobody who can bring on the clouds like somebody wringing his or her hands and trying to probe your depth of pain so they can share some of it."

"Note that these are small *l* and small *c* and not the partisan types you hung around with in Ottawa," Tim said. "I doubt that those types ever crack a smile."

"Oh yeah, they would if somebody from another party slipped on a banana peel. But I exaggerate – I know people from all the parties and not all of them are grim."

"Well, it's interesting," Tim said. "Because the stereotype is conservatives would like only traditional jokes while liberals are more flexible and open to new ideas, so they'd like their humour unconventional. The article says conservatives 'are supposed to be more rigid and less sophisticated but they liked even complex humour more.'"

"That doesn't surprise me at all," Hazel said while setting my carafe and a small mayonnaise jar on the table. I don't know whether it's liberal or conservative humour, but Hazel gets a chuckle out of surprising me almost daily with drinking instruments that are not traditionally used for wine. "Look at John McCain when he was running for the presidency down south. I'd say that choosing Sarah Palin as his running mate was very complex humour indeed."

"I've met a few Conservatives who are rigid," I said.

"Not around here," Hazel said and went back to the bar and her iPod.

It was then that Four-eyed Tom walked in and joined us at the table. He was laughing and we wondered why.

"I just saw Old Rutherford slip in the mud and fall on his ass," he said. "Haven't seen anything that funny in a long time."

"So would you describe yourself as a small *l* liberal or small *c* conservative, Tom?" Tim asked him.

"I think I'm still Social Credit," Tom said, "but they disappeared so I don't know what I am except I vote for the Progressive Conservatives in Alberta and the Conservatives in Ottawa."

"We'll put you down in the unconventional category," Tim told Tom, who looked pleased but confused, and opened his crossword puzzle book.

"I wonder how Purvis would label himself?"

"You can ask him when he arrives but my guess is he'll say rancher, which is a whole different set of politics. That's a subject that a political science student could write a PhD thesis on." I looked to see if Hazel was coming with Tom's two mugs and she was. She handed me a thimble.

"I was thinking that might be more appropriate for sissy juice," she said. "And by the way, I'd call myself a liberal."

"*Very* liberal, Hazel," I said, and she gave me a wink.

"Anyway, this will probably make your friends in the Press Gallery in Ottawa rethink their stereotypes. They won't be able to fill space by referring to the Conservatives in everything they write as humourless."

"I think after Stephane Dion they might have already had their rethink," I replied.

Purvis walked in and settled into his chair. "Did you guys hear that Sarah Palin says she'll look at running for the presidency in 2012? Geez, if that isn't a joke I don't know what is. She'll probably choose God as her running mate."

"I'd put Purvis down as a conservative," I told Tim. "He appreciates absurdist humour and irony."

Perley arrived a few minutes later and after tapping Hazel on the shoulder to get her attention away from her bar top video game, joined us at the table.

"Did you guys hear about the dyslexic dog who thought he was God?" he asked.

Four-eyed Tom stared blankly at Perley while the rest of us chuckled. Tim and I made a mental note to move Tom over to the liberal category.

Mad Dogs and Austrians

"Well, the researchers have proof of what I've been telling you guys for years," Hazel said as she began loading the table. "You old hounds are more kin to your dogs than to your families."

She handed me a clipping from the Calgary Herald which was out of Vienna via *Agence France-Presse* in Chicago. I mention this rather meandering path the story took before reaching The Just One More Saloon as a salute to Canada's ever-alert news gathering and dispensing industry. Vienna is quite distant from Manyberries.

I read the article while awaiting the arrival of Big Tim Little, Purvis, Perley and Four-eyed Tom to convene the December 10th Official Officers Cocktail Hour.

I arrived earlier than usual so I could select the day's topic because news reports said Michael Ignatieff was about to be confirmed as leader of the Liberal Party of the 416 area code. Bob Rae and the other contenders had withdrawn, leaving Ignatieff to wear the crown, or carry the can, whichever way you looked at it. Depending on how things turned out, Ignatieff was my choice as topic because I wanted to ask how he could expect us to support him if he'd never taken the time to visit Manyberries. Not that we would support him even if he did because we are, after all, in Alberta, where by custom, community standards and complacency we must always vote Conservative. When we don't, we mark our ballots for the Green or New Democratic parties to get people worrying that it might be contagious. Now I had further ammunition because I was almost certain that I had read somewhere that Ignatieff had visited Vienna.

The article Hazel gave me was headlined "Dogs feel envy, reject unequal treatment, study says."

"These are probably Canadian, or maybe New Democratic Party dogs," I yelled at Hazel, which wasn't necessary because she had remained standing beside me while I read the article.

"I would have said Manyberries dogs, based on too much time observing the behaviour of their humans," she said and returned to the bar.

The article said dogs can feel a simple form of envy and respond with petulance to unequal treatment. "Course, they could also be backbench Members of Parliament dogs in any party," I mused aloud.

Big Tim arrived first and I handed him the clipping and said that Ignatieff was my choice for first topic and the dog study had to be number two.

When the other three arrived, Tim explained to them that researchers in Vienna found, after surveying 29 dogs, all of them would refuse to shake a paw, after doing it a few times, if they saw another dog get a treat for doing it and they didn't get a treat. "But they don't care if the other dog gets a better treat," Tim said, "like a piece of sausage if the petulant dog only gets a piece of bread."

"If a dog saw the one beside him get a treat for offering his paw but he didn't get one, it'd only take a couple of tries before the first dog refused to go through the motions again. Makes sense to me," Tim said. "Why shake a paw if you don't get a treat like the other dog did?"

"Dogs are conservative free-enterprisers," Perley said. "They're not going to work for nothing."

"If it was my Tom, he'd just wait until the humans went away and then he'd eat the other dog, so he'd get both treats," Purvis said. His dog, Three-eyed Tom, is probably the biggest dog in the world. He's certainly the biggest dog anybody in Manyberries ever saw. He got his name because he has a spot right between his eyes that from a distance resembles a third eye. We gave him that name so Four-eyed Tom wouldn't be confused if we were in conversation about our various dogs. Three-eyed Tom, it has been suggested, might be the result of a perverted affair between one of the bigger breeds of dog and a Shetland pony. We're not certain what caused Four-eyed Tom.

"The researchers should have come here," Four-eyed Tom said, "because we've got a lot more than 29 dogs in Manyberries, maybe almost as many dogs as humans."

The official federal census population of Manyberries is about a hundred and Tom was correct in his estimate of the size of the dog population.

Tim read the last paragraph of the news story that quoted the lead researcher, Friederike Range of the University of Vienna. "It was not the presence of the second dog, but the fact that the partner received the food that was responsible for the change in the subjects' behaviour."

"Next thing you know they'll be giving humans the same test," Perley said. "They should come to Canada because there's no population on earth where you can find a heavier concentration of the envious and petulant."

"While we're on the subject of envy and petulance, what do you guys think of Michael Ignatieff?" I asked, which I thought was a subtle segue over to my choice of topic.

"I just saw him on television before I came over," Purvis reported, "and he had some pretty good things to say about the West. Said he liked our blue skies and some other stuff. He'd just been elected leader by the other MPs in Ottawa."

"He's never visited Manyberries," I said, "which weighs heavily against him finding any votes here. I think I read somewhere that he might have visited Vienna, and he's spent most of his life in other countries."

"Some day I'd like to visit Vienna," Four-eyed said without looking up from his crossword book. "They've got buildings over there that are even older than the Ranchmen's."

Hazel returned, pushing a wheeled serving cart that she had picked up at a flea market. "This is a hell of a lot easier on the back when I have to serve you old dogs," she said. She served me first while the others glowered impatiently, enviously and petulantly, waiting for her to put their stuff in front of them. "Why do you always serve him first?" Purvis asked her and she ignored him.

"The media say Ignatieff will give our guy a run for his money," Tim said. In Manyberries, Stephen Harper is "our guy"—we have to pause to explain that whenever somebody from another province visits. Nobody can recall that ever happening, however.

"Well, I feel some sympathy for Bob Rae," Perley said. "He's too old to wait around for another shot at it."

"If Rae had won, we'd have had a whole different political landscape in a few years," Hazel said. "Either the Liberal party or the New Democratic Party would have disappeared because he would have destroyed one or the other." I felt somewhat petulant because she had just advanced a theory that I had concocted that very morning.

"How so?" Tim asked. "Because the Conservatives would have won every seat in Ontario?"

"No," she said, "he would have either dragged so many votes away from the NDP that they disappeared or scared so many votes away to the Conservatives that the Liberals disappeared." Now I was really petulant because I had planned to postulate exactly that scenario. I was envious too because the other guys all told her they admired her political acumen.

"Anyway, about this dog study," I said.

Singin' the Blooze

"Did you hear what those rubes up in Edmonton are doing?" Hazel asked as she set my instruments in front of me. "These guys are acting less like jetsetters and more and more like tractor pilots."

"What've they done now? No wait, let me guess. They've banned same sex conversations."

"That'll come next," Hazel said. "No, they're bringing in new legislation that will set the prices we charge for booze. On top of that, they're going to regulate so-called happy hours. I wouldn't put it past them to tell bar owners they're going to have to open every day with a Bible reading."

"Conservatives don't set prices," I said. "They don't get into the business of business. Only New Democrats and Liberals and Bible thumpers do that."

"Nobody said those clowns are Conservatives," Hazel snorted. "Here, take a look at this," and she handed me a story headlined 'Alberta targets cheap booze specials.' I got it off the Canoe website."

"It says here," I told my cocktail hour companions, "Stelmach and his bunch are now dictating how much bars can charge for drinks. A bottle of beer can't sell for less than $2.75, pints have to be $3.20 or more and wine can't sell for less than $1.75 per glass. Geez, Hazel, does this mean you'll be lowering the price of wine?" She gave me a not-so-gentle pat on the back of the head and said probably, but not until pigs take flight.

"That sort of sounds communistic to me," Purvis said. "It sure isn't free enterprise."

"Not so much communistic as slowly advancing the nanny state," Big Tim Little said. "I think what we've got here is a busybody government run by the descendants of the Women's Christian

Temperance Union. My old Dad told me they were the most obnoxious bunch of old biddies you'd ever meet."

"I had a grandmother I didn't like who was one of those," Perley said. "She'd come to visit and look in all the cupboards to make sure my old man wasn't keeping a bottle hidden somewhere. That was why he kept it in the woodshed."

"Says here," I continued reading, "that Solicitor General Fred Lindsay says 'there's always going to be people who drink too much and we want to discourage that activity.' If that's not a page out of the WCTU manual, nothing is."

"Next thing you know they'll be passing a law that says we can't brew up our own liquor," Four-eyed Tom told us. "They'll tell me I have to get rid of my still."

"They did that about a hundred years ago, Tom," I told him, "and it's still illegal to own one."

"Well, nobody told me," he said, "and besides they have to find it first."

"Maybe we should join Saskatchewan," Purvis said, "or better yet, Montana."

"Montana would be the better choice," Tim said. "People there were as resistant to prohibition as Americans anywhere. No way they'd put up with this sort of clammy-handed, spoon-feeding, keyhole-peeping style of government."

"Tim, if you can remember verbatim what you just said, I think you've got the makings of a fiery good editorial for the Bald Prairie Tattler," I said. "Or maybe a guest appearance on some talk show."

"You know what we could do is load up at home before we come here," Four-eyed Tom suggested. "We'd have a few at home, come here and have our usual number and nobody would ever know. It'd be our own secret happy hour."

"Let the revolution commence," I said.

Wither the Queen

"So Queen Liz is tightening her belt," Tim said when he joined us for a mid-December session of the longest running cocktail hour in the history of Manyberries. No other saloon in Manyberries can lay claim to being the headquarters of what Hazel calls the most agonizing and painful way she could ever imagine spending her early evenings. The fact there is no other saloon in Manyberries makes it no less a remarkable and historic record.

"Yep, according to the internet the old girl has sent word out to the whole royal family that ostentatious behaviour this Christmas is to be avoided. She wants them all to set an example by recognizing that they've got hard times over there."

"Over there?" Purvis snorted. "Just look outside – with the wind, it's minus 40. They think *they've* got hard times?"

Tim explained that it was the economy that Queen Elizabeth the Two was concerned about, not their weather, but Purvis wasn't impressed and wondered where she was when we had the mad cow crisis. I think he's what you call an agnostic monarchist.

"She even wore the same pink dress out in public twice," Tim informed us, "and apparently that's not something she's ever done. You've gotta admire a woman who'd do that."

"My old grandma wore the same house dress for close to 30 years," Perley said, "every day of the week except when she wore an old robe on washing day."

"Well, she was a woman who deserved admiration as well," Tim said.

"Not my admiration," Perley replied. "She was the meanest-spirited old hag I ever met. Even my father, her own son, didn't like her."

I told them I was going to follow the example Queen Elizabeth was setting by using only paper plates at our pre-Christmas party at my house. They reminded me they'd never seen anything but paper plates at that party in all the years they've attended. I explained it was a belt-tightening tradition because it saves on dish soap. Four-eyed Tom said he did something similar by using one paper plate three times a day for a week before discarding it but it was because he hated washing dishes. Hazel shuddered and went back to the bar to wash her hands.

"Well, I'd just say the Queen is more in touch with her people than our politicians are with us, if she's doing that," Tim said. "She even insists that leftovers from her banquets have to be used in some way. I'll lay you odds that nobody in Edmonton or Ottawa would ever dream of having banquet leftovers the next day."

I told them that when I lived in Ottawa I never, not once, put a wine bottle down the garbage chute until I had tipped it into a glass for a few hours to make sure nothing was wasted. They conceded that there might have been *one* guy there who had Queenly tendencies. I assured them there was a hell of a lot more than one.

"You guys should come up with a list of austerity measures and sacrifices you'll make so Manyberries will be a role model for the world," Hazel said when she returned. "Take Purvis, for starters. He could walk over here instead of driving that four-wheel-drive tank he calls a pickup."

"If you think I'm gonna walk 500 yards in minus 40 temperatures, you're talking to the wrong cowboy," he informed her. "I won't even do it in the summer so I'm sure as hell not gonna start now."

"You could drive around and pick us all up," Four-eyed Tom said. "I'd save a bundle if I left my flatbed at home."

Purvis told him, rather austerely I thought, he'd do it if we all chipped in two dollars each to cover fuel and wear and tear. Four-eyed went back to his crossword puzzle.

"Well, I'm going to wear my last year's Christmas outfit," Hazel said. "That will be my austerity measure and not just because I couldn't find a nicer one." The tee-shirt Hazel had worn the previous Christmas was severely scooped with a rhinestone Christmas tree and an inebriated Santa leering out from behind it. The words in the balloon coming out of his mouth had him saying, "Be naughty or else." I told her she could wear that tee-shirt any time she wanted because I really and truly admired her austerity.

There was more in the story about royal frugality and how it wasn't likely anybody would see any of the young royals getting crapulent on expensive booze at fancy nightclubs. The consensus at the table was we wouldn't be following the example set by the young royals, except for the part about fancy nightclubs and expensive booze because it's too far to drive to Calgary.

"You know, this setting an example thing is a good idea," Perley said. "So this Christmas Eve I'm not going to buy the last round for the table before we go home."

The consensus around the table was that it's not a good idea to get carried away with setting austerity examples.

Blue Spanish Running Shoe

Big Tim Little called me at home to say he would be at The Just One More Saloon early so he could have first dibs on the topic for the day. He warned me that Four-eyed Tom wanted to discuss how a transsexual in Spain gave birth to twins in the middle of a sex change procedure and Purvis told him to talk to me because anybody who spent as much time in Ottawa as I did would no doubt have engaged in many conversations on just this topic.

"What's your item?" I asked Tim. "And by the way, was there any mention of Barcelona in the sex change story?"

"Why do you ask about Barcelona?"

"I was thinking about Fawlty Towers and the headwaiter. They always explained his behaviour by pointing out he was from Barcelona."

"My topic is a quadruple murderer who sued the feds for $6,000 because the prison didn't replace his worn-out running shoes and he injured his knee as a result."

"Maybe you could just explain that I left really early for Palm Springs," I said. "Not to suggest that your topic isn't worthy of discussion but quadruple murderers and transsexual miracle births are a bit weighty for me, at least in the first three hours."

"They know you never go away before Christmas because you don't want to miss Hazel's Santa Claus tee-shirt," he said. "Anyway, what have *you* got?"

"Mine's about a terrorist who hid a pound of high explosives with a detonator in his rectum in an attempt to assassinate some Saudi Arabian counter-terrorist operative."

"They must have very well maintained roads in Saudi Arabia," Tim said.

"What the hell do roads have to do with terrorists running around with bombs in their bums?"

"Well, imagine what it would be like to drive on the roads around here with that kind of set-up. Hell, you'd hit the first pothole between here and Onefour and boom, an even bigger pothole. You might get one or two unlucky gophers but that's about all."

We decided in the end to hit The Just One More right after lunch so our two topics would lead the agenda. We figured by the time ours were exhausted we might be in shape to tackle the transsexual. I forewarned Tim that I would attempt to clarify things for Four-eyed by telling him to imagine that his old flatbed truck had two transmissions so as to help him understand what confronts a transsexual in today's society. You put one in gear and run to put the other in gear and then sit there, going nowhere because they're working against each other.

Tim said all he wanted to do was get Purvis and Perley going on the rights of criminals versus the rights of the rest of us. He was armed with the fact that the prisoner in question had ordered, and didn't get in a timely fashion, new extra-wide Size 13 New Balance running shoes and that's why he sued.

"Gotta figure those shoes would cost a small fortune, a lot more than those high top canvas sneakers Perley wears and maybe more than Purvis pays for his riding boots."

The judge awarded the prisoner the cash because of "the appalling delay" in getting the new shoes to the quadruple murderer and further for "malfeasance in public office", a provision that allows citizens to go after public servants for intentional abuses of power. There apparently was no mention of how a quadruple murderer who is also an American qualifies as a citizen, but that could just be me splitting hairs.

We decided we had better meet at noon to be absolutely certain our chosen topics would lead the agenda but when we arrived Perley and Purvis were already there and engaged in the topic they had selected. It was about Ontario Premier Dalton McGuinty suing tobacco manufacturers for $50 billion to recover health care costs related to smoking going back to 1955.

Perley was insisting that McGuinty should also include the tobacco farmers in his suit, while Purvis was adamant in advancing the opposite position, that agriculture always gets unfairly blamed for every little problem.

"If he sues the farmers," Purvis was arguing as we took our chairs, "the bugger'll be coming after the ranchers next for cholesterol in beef."

Perley agreed it was a slippery slope that McGuinty was on but said suing them would be easier than suing all the people who smoked and thereby created their own health problems.

It was three hours after the regular start time of 5:00 when we finally got around to Four-eyed Tom's item about the transsexual in Spain giving birth. He passed around a clipping from the Calgary Herald which his thumb prints hadn't obscured all that much. "So this is a woman who wants to be a man," he said, "and is getting an operation to get rid of the girl stuff and another one after that so she'll have what it takes to be a man." We all nodded our understanding. Hazel stood with a full tray of empties, not wanting to miss this one.

"So, her girl friend can't have any more babies, so this first one stops the operation stuff and she has twins. Now she's going to get the rest of the operation and then they're going to get married." Again we all nodded that we were following Tom on this.

"So I'm wondering," Tom said, "when those kids grow up, which one they will call Mom and which one Dad?"

"I think, Tom," Tim said, "that you'd call these modern or new age parents, and they'll probably insist that the kids call them by their first names."

The Doggie Doggie Doo

"Did you hear the announcement of the biggest lie of the year?" Tim asked as I moaned my way down into my chair. I shook my head and looked longingly over at Hazel who was shimmying to the music in her iPod and playing a video game. I was hoping that I wasn't hoping in vain that she'd notice my presence and shimmy her way to the table with a loaded tray.

"They've got this Liars Club down in Burlington, Milwaukee," Tim explained, "and every January they announce the winning lie for the previous year."

"Let me guess," I said, "It *was* beer that made Milwaukee phlegmatic?"

"No, but that would be a good one to enter in next year's contest. Or you could try to work up a few really tall tales – cripes, any guy who spent as long as you did in Ottawa would be a sure bet to come up with a winner."

"What was the lie?" Four-eyed Tom asked. "Maybe it'll come in handy sometime."

"My grandson is the most persuasive liar I have ever met," Tim said. "By the time he was two years old, he could dirty his diaper and make his mother believe somebody else had done it."

Four-eyed Tom sat quietly and patiently waiting for Tim to tell the lie that won the contest until Tim explained that that *was* the lie.

Tom didn't laugh and explained that whenever his old dog, Arnold, has accidents in the house he looks around in surprise as if wondering what kind of dog would do something like that and where it had gone.

Tim said in the story about the Burlington Liars Club it was mentioned that the previous year's winner had also won 12 years earlier when he told about strong winter winds in Wisconsin. He had reported that the wind was so strong that it blew away his brother's bald spot and left him with a full head of hair. Tom didn't laugh at that one either because he is a bit sensitive about bald jokes, being three-quarters bald and all. And you haven't experienced wind if you've only visited Manyberries on the two or three days when it isn't blowing.

"Here's a whopper for you," I said. "Calgary City Council appears poised to make an intelligent decision."

"They wouldn't even believe that in Wisconsin, let alone Calgary," Tim said, "and anyway, the secret to a good lie is that it has to sound possible but in no way believable. So there goes your lie."

"Well, they've approved a study on how the city can reduce the millions and millions of plastic grocery bags that go to the dump every year. A rough estimate puts the number of those things at nearly 800 million annually."

"And what doesn't get buried gets blown down here," Tim said. "You can't drive a mile without seeing one hanging on a barb wire fence."

"I don't think they're considering it as a civic beautification project for Manyberries, but hey, it could be a side benefit."

"I hate those things," Tom said. "Last year I crawled across a mile of prairie because I thought what I saw was an antelope's rump. Turned out to be one of those bags."

"But the Calgary Herald says there are some questions Calgarians will want answered before they support a ban on the bags. People are wondering how they'll pick up their dogs' droppings when they take them out for a walk."

"What do you mean pick up the droppings?" Purvis asked.

"Well, there are bylaws in some cities that force dog owners to stoop and scoop, in other words, clean up the piles their dogs leave."

"You mean people actually go around town up there picking up dog droppings?" Perley was sceptical … no, he was disbelieving.

"Like the guys carrying shovels who walk behind the horses in parades?" Tom wondered. "Geez, first of all, who takes a dog out for a walk when you can just let him out the back door? And who'd carry a shovel if you were out with your dog? All I ever carry when I'm out with my dog is my shotgun."

"They don't use shovels, or if they do, they're probably Martha Stewart-approved garden trowels, but most of them just use their hands," I explained. "At least the ones I used to see up there in Calgary or down in Ottawa."

"You mean they actually use their bare hands to actually pick up what their dogs left? What kind of people are those?" Four-eyed Tom was shaking his head in disgust.

"No, they use their shopping bags to hold whatever they scoop up after the dog."

"In there with the groceries? You'd think they'd have laws against that, even in the city." For the sake of clarification, Four-eyed Tom doesn't visit too many cities and when he does drive all the way to Calgary, he walks Arnold around a city-owned golf course late at night or very early in the morning. He explained that his sister-in-law gets pretty impatient when the old dog has accidents on her living room rug.

"No, Tom, the bags are empty; they use bags they've carried the groceries in as mitts for the pickup. Then they toss them in the garbage when they get home."

"It'd take two of me to pick up after Tom," Purvis said. He wasn't referring to Four-eyed Tom in that comment; he was talking about his dog Three-eyed Tom, the biggest dog anybody ever saw.

"What's that place where they have the liar's club?" Tom asked Tim, who told him it was in Wisconsin.

"You should write to them and tell them that we have a guy here who tells even better lies," Four-eyed said, nodding at me. "He could win that contest easy with that story about people walking around with grocery bag mittens picking up dog crap."

Three Clowns in Coalition

One of the hot and ongoing topics in Manyberries started way back in December, 2008 when a flood of reports out of Ottawa, more like a tsunami than a mere flood, rolled across the country about three political parties forming a coalition to replace the governing Conservatives. The upheaval was equal in magnitude, perhaps greater, than you might experience from a bucketful of bad clams. Certain segments of the Manyberries population were ready to take to the streets in protest until they checked the thermometer.

It popped up again just the other day when some columnist in Ottawa, 54 short paragraphs into his yawner, mentioned in passing that it wasn't likely to be reborn as a plot to topple the government. That was enough, however, to stir certain segments of the population to consider taking to the streets in protest until they remembered the wind was blowing so hard it would have shredded the placards, if anybody had any.

But this columnist's reminder triggered some reminiscing about those foreboding days when Stephane Dion, Jack Layton and Gilles Duceppe signed a letter to the Governor General in which they stated they were prepared to replace the governing party.

Unbeknownst to Mr. Dion, another coup was taking shape in other corridors that would soon see him replaced by Michael Ignatieff, who had signed the letter to the GG but changed his mind later, no doubt after hearing the roars carried on the wind from Manyberries.

Back then there had been rallies for and against the coalition from coast to coast and to that other coast they always mention.

So it was a dark and stormy December Saturday in 2008 when I arrived, later than usual, at The Just One More Saloon.

I had been exchanging e-mails with friends in Ottawa about the rallies being held to either support the Conservatives or protest the coalition.

A friend had wondered if the Calgary rally had been a success, having assumed, wrongly, that I would have participated. I replied that instead of rallying I sorted my socks by colour. I do that in December rather than January when our month-long New Year's Eve celebration occupies our waking hours. Besides, sorting socks has as much impact on what happens in Ottawa as attending a rally.

Big Tim, Perley, Purvis, Four-eyed Tom and Hazel were there along with an assortment of ranchers, cowboys, Hutterites and other denizens of the remote, all at their chosen tables. My carafe and a jelly jar with a Christmas motif were waiting for me. Hazel had very thoughtfully also put my Saturday lunch (beer and tomato juice) on the table.

"Thought you'd be in Calgary waving placards and rallying against the coalition," Big Tim said.

"I liked your idea of having a rally here," Purvis said, "but got busy so I called Bert in Regina to tell him that he and Fannie should demonstrate outside Ralph Goodale's office."

"I promised to watch a demonstration on television this morning," Perley told me, "but there was a Riders of the Purple Sage movie on and I never got to the news channels."

"I had to let my dog out in the backyard," Four-eyed Tom told me, "and besides I don't do demonstrations."

I had a vague recollection of trying to persuade the membership that as citizens we were obligated to lend our voices to the national uproar over the machinations in Ottawa.

"I thought that up until 9:30 your argument that we rally to support Stephen was very convincing," Hazel told me. "But then, around 10:30 when you swung your considerable influence over to the coalition, I was ready to catch a plane out of Medicine Hat to fly to Ottawa and hug Jack Layton."

I had told them that in a democracy, we have to seriously consider the arguments on both sides of important issues before making our decision. "It is how the politically engaged operate," I had said in fully lubricated pontificatory flight. "We listen carefully to what the other sides are saying and then immediately forget what they said. That's how Parliament has always operated and you don't mess with tradition."

I handed a folded sheet of paper to Hazel and told her I had written a song for her. She reminded me that she knew the lyrics to every song that had ever been written and didn't need any schoolboy lame attempt to emulate the masters. Once, on a very bitterly cold night when I was leaving, she sang a bit about button up your overcoat and that was enough to warm me all the way home.

"This is a shaky attempt at satire," I said. "Clumsy, but I had fun messing around with it."

"It's nice that you have fun messing around with something," she said and went back to the bar with the empties and my song sheet.

"Well, if I hadn't voted for the Green Party as a joke, I'd be mad as a hornet if those three yahoos did get together and throw Stephen out of office," Purvis told us. "And I didn't know that Elizabeth May would be getting a buck ninety-five a year just because I voted for her party."

"They should go out and raise their own money and not get it from us taxpayers," Four-eyed Tom said. "That's another reason why I didn't vote."

Tom's contributions are often so mystifying that it sometimes takes days to comprehend, or to forget, what he said.

Hazel returned and gave me a pat on the head. "This isn't bad; in fact I'd give you an A for effort on this one." She yelled at the joint to give her some quiet and said she wasn't sure she could do it like Audrey Hepburn but she'd give it a try. Unlike the rest of us, Hazel can actually sing on key and, when she does sing, she charms us all.

> Three clowns in coalition
> Each one seeking Sussex bliss
> Three hapless losers together
> And not one will the voters bless
>
> Three hearts in alliance
> Each heart longing for that home
> Ahh, to stand at that mansion's window
> Tossing restless voters meatless bones
>
> Three clowns in ménage a trois
> See their foreheads sweat and shine
> When they drive by that house on Sussex
> You can hear their dentures grind.
>
> Duceppe: le faire le notre (make it ours)
> Layton: make it mine! (le fair le mien)
> Dion: non, le faire le mien (no, make it mine!!!)

Written in late 2008, this song will be held in abeyance until such time as Michael Ignatieff decides to go back on the signature he already went back on the first time, and dives into a coalition. I probably won't even need to make changes, apart from replacing Dion's name with his.

Max the Knife

I had tried to get to The Just One More Saloon well before the official commencement of the Manyberries Official Officers Cocktail Hour but was delayed by The Young and the Restless. Victor was in jail on a trumped up charge and he was blaming Nikki for framing him and I didn't want to lose track of the narrative on the off chance that I might miss the next day's instalment. I could have gone earlier to watch the whole hour with Hazel, who bears a remarkable resemblance to Nikki, but feared she might twig to my secret viewing habits. I was disappointed to find Perley and Purvis already settled in, which meant my choice for topic was going to be second and perhaps number three on the agenda.

Purvis had arrived before Perley so the topic was going to be controls on knives in Japan. The government over there was meeting to consider limiting access to knives with blades of a certain length. Purvis was likening it to gun control in Canada and arguing that if they did pass a law like that, they'd be singling out people who peel carrots or apples and giving a pass to criminals who'd ignore the knife registration law. The blade length limit the Japanese were considering was 12.7 centimetres. Purvis wanted to know what that meant in a length he could understand. I held up my right hand with middle finger extended and told him that 12.7 centimetres was slightly longer than that. He replied that he no longer wanted to discuss a Japanese ban on knives.

"Hell, my skinning knife blade is longer than that," he said, "Those Japanese are talking about something the size of my castrating knife. Isn't worth talking about over here."

Big Tim Little arrived, followed by Four-eyed Tom. Neither had their own suggestions for topics but agreed that a knife registration law in

Japan wasn't worth discussing in Manyberries where even the women know that size matters when it comes to knives. Hazel observed that it wasn't just knives, but nobody except me was interested in her theory.

Perley's offering was a story out of Ottawa about a 25-year-old guy with a lengthy record for drug possession and assaults. He had pleaded guilty to robbery to avoid a trial in which the Crown was unable to produce the key witness because she had disappeared.

"The bottom line to this story," Perley said, "was the judge told this guy that he should turn his life around or one day he was going to receive a lengthy sentence. Now, here you have a guy who's got a record as long as your arm and he gets away with this and all the judge does is say he'd better watch out and maybe not pout because Santa Claus might not come to his house some Christmas. What the hell is wrong with the legal system?"

Four-eyed Tom was already deep into his crossword puzzle book and didn't respond, and Big Tim just sort of sighed and shook his head. "Maybe the judge thought the prisons are too full, or maybe such a stern talking-to would convince this guy to walk the straight and narrow," he said. "Either way, it means we've either gotta change the laws or better yet, the judges."

"Well, you know what Mahatamahootma Ghandi said," Purvis offered. "He said: 'Among the many misdeeds of British rule in India, history will look upon the act of depriving a whole nation of arms as the blackest.' No truer words were ever spoken."

Perley and Four-eyed Tom nodded agreement while Tim and I sat with eyes wide in silent amazement. Tim finally broke the silence when he asked Purvis if he had been reading Ghandi's works.

"No, I saw that in a National Post some guy left on that table over there," Purvis said and waved at Hazel to bring us more ammunition while they all turned to me, wondering what my chosen topic was.

I had read an article on Canoe from the Sun Newspapers Parliamentary Bureau that detailed how much taxpayers would be dinged for the Christmas lights display in the national capital. It said the cost of stringing the lights was over $139,000 and electricity added another $34,000 to the tab.

"Holy crapoli, that's probably more than we spend in a whole year on light bulbs and electricity in Manyberries," Perley exclaimed and thanked Hazel for her delivery of our Christmas spirits.

"So you think that Stephen should pull the switch on that to save us all that money?" Tim asked.

"No, it's an interesting story but I think it's a bit of a nitpicker. I loved seeing those lights at the House of Commons, both on the outside and the inside. I don't care if it costs twice that much and I hope they never stop doing it."

"I was in Ottawa once, the first time I met him," Purvis said and pointed a thumb in my direction. "It wasn't at Christmas but I still admired the way they lit up Parliament Hill at night. It's a grand sight and makes even a guy from the West feel Canadian."

Tim said he hadn't known that Purvis and I had met before Manyberries. I don't remember but Purvis swears we did when he was there as part of a group that raise cows for a living and they were meeting Members of Parliament. As he tells it, they ended their week at the now defunct National Press Club of Canada on a Friday night and I was on the public address system to welcome and introduce them. That might well have been possible on a Friday night at the Press Club but only a few people, other than the ones who raise cows, would remember even the next morning, let alone a few years later.

"So what's it like when they put up the Christmas lights?" Hazel asked. "I've only seen bits of it on television."

I asked them if they knew that song with the lyrics 'A Kind of a Hush', and explained that's what it used to feel like to me. Inside the Centre Block, the halls are dark but they're lined with Christmas trees and no matter what the politicians might be yelling at each other in the Commons, the mood changes when they walk past all those lights and decorations. It's magical, I said, even people who hate each other's partisan guts feel it and become friendly when they pass in the halls.

"This story about the cost of the lights," I said, "will have the usual and perpetually disgruntled set bitching about extravagance in Ottawa without knowing what it feels like."

"Do you miss it," Hazel asked, "being there at Christmas?"

I told them of one December night when we headed over to a little bistro across the river in what was then known as Hull, and still is today as far as I'm concerned. It was one of the few places where they still allowed smoking and was a favourite spot for couples in love and that was one of the reasons I loved it. Smokers occupied tables on one side of the room and non-smokers were on the other side about six feet away. Back in those days they were far more civilized than the restaurants on the Ontario side.

"So, in this room, you had Members of Parliament from all parties tossing greetings and jokes back and forth, sending glasses of wine or cognac to each other and not even a hint that they were opponents over anything."

I said they should leave the Christmas lights and decorations up year round. "And keep that little bistro in Hull open forever, for good measure."

Bad Dogs and Englishmen

"I think if I had to live in England, I'd go stark raving mad," Hazel told me as I settled into my favourite chair. "It's no bloody wonder Canadians are a whining, snivelling, self-righteous, not to forget namby-pamby bunch of softies, considering the influence the Brits have had on us."

"Do I sense an editorial approaching at great speed?" I asked. "Or are you still getting up early on Sundays to watch Coronation Street? Either way, if you bring me a carafe I'll pay rapt attention."

"Or maybe it's just the media," she said and slapped two printouts down in front of me. I couldn't read them immediately because I had to watch her saunter back to the bar, which is another of the many perquisites of regular attendance at The Just One More Saloon.

After she got behind the bar I scanned the two sheets, which were about an "Incident at Sandringham", the private estate of Queen Elizabeth in Norfolk, England. Apparently, paparazzi had photographed Prince Edward, the Queen's third son, waving a stick at two dogs fighting over a dead pheasant. The pheasant was dead because somebody had shot it, which is an activity enjoyed year round by the Royals and others who can afford it. In Manyberries we can only shoot pheasants in October and early November because we're not Royal. And we won't pay to go to one of those places where they raise pheasants so people who can afford it can shoot them any time they want.

Hazel returned with my wine and told me what really frosted her was that it was all "alleged" because the photos showed "what appeared to be the stick in Edward's hand coming very close to the fighting dogs" and the uproar over "what might have been" actual contact. "They're hedging, making up a story about something that might have happened. When did they start reporting on what didn't happen but could have happened?"

When I was seven years old my cocker spaniel got in a fight with a bigger dog and to save him I waded and in and grabbed his collar. I still have the scar on my left thumb where one of the combatants bit it clear through. That was when I learned that a stick was a safer way to save a dog than personal intervention. I have a sneaking hunch Prince Edward was either taught that or learned it the way I did.

Hazel picked up one of the sheets and read a line from it: "Hitting a dog is a pathetic, cowardly and vicious act … a truly sickening example." She then asked me if I'd ever been up close to a dog fight. I stuck my left thumb up and nodded. I think she took that as encouragement to continue. "The guy who made that comment speaks for the League Against Cruel Sports over there. He says hunting dogs are so well trained that a simple tone of voice command should separate them. Probably the closest he's ever come to dogs is Chihuahuas and you could use toilet paper to separate those little rats."

"But it is the media's silly season, Hazel. They have to have something to fill the spaces between the Boxing Day ads. Not that there's that much space to fill these days because they're shrinking the pages and reducing the font size."

"But it gets worse," she said. "They go back to every incident involving the Royal Family and animals almost to when they were still beheading each other, the Royals that is, not the animals. In one story they remember how Queen Elizabeth was photographed wringing the neck of a pheasant. In the other one the writer says critics attacked the Queen – and at this point Hazel started reading directly from the printout – 'after she used her bare hands to kill a pheasant that didn't die immediately after being shot during a royal outing.' Hell, when I read years and years ago that she had wrung a pheasant's neck, that was when I thought she was the sort of Queen I'd like to have as a friend."

"I can just hear them around the newsroom screaming that she scrambles around on her hands and knees at Sandringham with her Corgis, grabbing pheasants to strangle."

"How many pheasant necks have you wrung?" Hazel asked me. I shrugged to indicate it was too many to count.

"Maybe I'll go hunting with you next year and take care of any necks that need wringing. You can write a news release saying 'Hazel Wrings Pheasant Necks' and maybe I'll be as famous as Elizabeth."

"Or be pegged as barbaric as a Queen," I said. "Remember, all of this crap comes from reporters, men and women, who squeal and jump up on chairs if they see a mouse."

"Are they what you call society reporters?"

"Yeah, I guess, if it's considered pejorative. Get me a dictionary and I'll find a few other names."

"But why would they change what they say from wringing a neck in the first story to killing a pheasant with her bare hands in the second one?"

"Because the writer of the second story doesn't know what he or she is even writing about, and besides, killing a pheasant with bare hands sounds even more cruel and gruesome than neck wringing. It's the media gone tabloid."

"Maybe they're just jealous that they weren't invited to join the Royals over the Christmas season at the palace," Hazel suggested.

"Yeah, some media people I've known believe that anyone who isn't media has no right to be richer, more content, happier or drunker than they are."

"I wonder if the Queen has contempt for the media?"

"No more than the rest of us."

"So when does this silly season end?"

"When there are no more trees."

The Bulls of Berkeley Square

"You know, guys, I think I've finally discovered the answer to what's been bothering us all this time," Purvis said as we opened what might have been the 14-hundred and 22nd session of the Manyberries Official Officers Cocktail Hour.

"How is it Celine Dion came to be a millionaire?" Big Tim Little asked.

"What's the real reason for Jack Layton and the New Democratic Party?" Perley suggested.

"What's the real reason for you guys?" Hazel said as she began loading the table.

"How come Stephen Harper won't lower the tax on beer?" Four-eyed Tom said. "Especially in times like these when people are suffering." Tom doesn't talk a whole lot but can go on at opera-length when it comes to why there should be no tax on beer or his favourite brand of cheap rye.

"Why do the provincial Progressive Conservatives in Edmonton call themselves Progressive?" I guessed.

"No, how to make Manyberries one of the world's capitals," Purvis said. "And how to create an industry here that brings people in from all over the world." He hauled out two sheets of paper that had come from a computer.

"Your grandsons been surfing the net again, Purvis?" I asked as he handed me the printouts. The story was off the CTV News website and was headlined "Nightingale droppings used in bizarre spa treatments".

"Yeah, those guys are wizards with that thing. One of them is 15 and the other guy is 17 and I guess they've met girls on this internet thing who are barely 18. Man, when I was young, an 18-year-old girl wouldn't look at a guy even a year younger. Anyway, I guess talking to girls on the internet will keep them out of trouble."

The story, and it was a story because it sure as hell wasn't news, went on at great length about how some beauty salons in New York are using nightingale droppings mixed with bran to give women facials.

"I don't think we have nightingales in Alberta, Purvis," I said. "You might have to settle for turkey vultures."

"No, it's the part about the bulls," he said. "That's right up our alley."

I read further and discovered that in London, England, women are getting their hair treated with bull semen. The protein and moisture, it said, revitalizes and repairs all types of hair.

"See, over in England, when they put bull semen on women's hair, they have to get it from bulls in Scotland," Purvis explained with even more enthusiasm than he usually displays when he's contemplating a sure-fire money-making scheme. "Now, if there's one thing we have plenty of around here, it's bull semen."

"And there's even more of another bunch of bull stuff around here," Hazel said. "Mountains of it every day around 5:00 pm except Sundays."

Purvis ignored her. "The way I see it, we could set up one of these beauty salons and offer bull semen treatments for women with damaged hair. There's a lot of them who dye their hair or who have dry frizzy hair like it says in that story who'd be coming here in droves."

"No doubt, there are a lot of women in Alberta who have dry frizzy hair," Hazel said. "But it's not all because of dye and treatments. We have a pretty dry and frizzy climate here and water you shouldn't drink or even use to wash your scanties. But if I was the owner of that New York salon I'd change the name to Florence of Nightingale and move it over to London near Berkeley Square."

"If we set up a salon here, in The Just One More Saloon, you could make a fortune selling them beer while they get their hair semened," Purvis told Hazel.

"Does it grow hair?" Four-eyed Tom asked. Some years back Tom went to Regina where he'd heard some doctor was doing hair transplants. He called it quits half-way through the first session because it hurt too much. He explained that he could stick forks in his head if he wanted pain and it wouldn't cost him anything. He now has five little tufts of hair in a row about two inches ahead of where his hairline is. A few more years and the tufts will be three inches ahead, sort of like five little soldiers standing out there as a rear guard for a retreating army.

"No, it treats *damaged* hair, but we could always *claim* that it stops hair loss. You can claim just about anything if you're selling shampoo."

"They used to say that sheep manure would grow hair," Tom said. It was a strong urge but I resisted and didn't ask him.

"Do you think women would know the difference between nightingale and pigeon poop?" Perley asked. "Because there's a big flock of pigeons in that old barn on the way to Orion."

"Geishas probably would but I can't picture too many of them coming all the way over from Japan, where they probably have a lot of nightingales," Hazel said. "But I don't think there's a Berkeley Square in Tokyo so we might have to give the parking lot a name."

The story said Geishas used the nightingale concoction to remove their heavy white makeup, which contained quantities of lead.

"The thing is, over in London they charge women 86 bucks per treatment. If we got a hundred women coming in every week just to get their hair done, that's 86 hundred bucks every six days. Do you know how much that would be per year?" Purvis looked around the table and up at Hazel. "Well I don't either but even split six ways it's a lot of cash. And then you've got Perley's pigeon droppings on top of that."

"Yeah, but who will you get to put their hands in that stuff?" Tom wondered. "I wouldn't, not even wearing my welding gloves."

"Another great idea down in flames," Hazel sympathized. "And just because the only beautician in Manyberries doesn't want the job."

The Mystery Writer

I was surprised to see Four-eyed Tom bent over our table writing in a lined exercise book and not in one of his crossword puzzle books. I knew he could write but didn't think he was good for more than one word at a time because that's generally about the limit of his conversational skills.

"What are you writing, Tom, your life story? Because if you are, you don't need a whole exercise book."

"I'm writing a mystery story," he said without looking up. He licked the pencil tip and feverishly wrote down two more words, which went beyond all my expectations.

"Well, there's a market for mystery stories out there. I'm busy with Ruth Rendell's latest and if I can't find anybody to replace her, maybe I'll read yours when you get it published."

"If I live long enough," I added to myself.

"This is a Canadian story," he informed me, "an incredible west coast mystery about missing feet. My book will solve The Mystery of the Missing Feet. I don't know how yet, but I'll find out near the end of the book."

"Are you talking about those feet that keep washing up on the B.C. coast? I asked. "Because that is a hell of a mystery and in the hands of an accomplished writer would probably make a good yarn."

"Exactly what I was thinking," he said and furrowed his brow as he searched for the exactly the right word to put down next. I was reading upside down so I'm not absolutely positive but I'm pretty sure the word he finally selected had two letters.

"Hazel left this story on the table for us to read," he said, "and I figured it was just the ticket to a great book."

"Probably will be," I yawned, "and if not that, at least something to occupy one's mind until the real thing comes along."

Hazel drifted over to the table with my carafe and, surprise, a real stemmed wine glass. I looked up warily to see what she might be up to but she was all innocence. "What, no Campbell's Soup can, hollowed-out coconut or something equally exotic?"

"I was distracted by that story Tom is reading. Not what he's writing but what he read to get started. It's about your idiot friends in the media."

"What, they're losing their feet now?"

"No, their vocabulary. Look at the headline."

I could see the headline upside down. It was something she'd pulled off the internet. The headline read "Another Grizzly Discovery on West Coast."

"I thought B.C. had an abundance of grizzlies," I said. "In fact, I know they have because I watched a film on them on the Discovery Channel the other day."

"It isn't about bears, it's about missing feet that people keep finding," Tom informed me.

It dawned on me then what was bothering Hazel, who is a sharp critic of lazy and/or incompetent journalism. Actually, Hazel is a sharp critic of a lot of things, so journalists shouldn't feel persecuted. Of course it wouldn't be a bad thing if they did.

"Let's hope they never have to write about tough, flexible tissue in bear carcasses," I said, "because you'll have headlines like Grisly Grizzle in Gristly Bears."

"Well, the other one that ticks me is when they interchange *reign* and *rein*," Hazel said. "Like long may Queen Elizabeth rein over us or how she reigned in one of her sons so as to spare the monarchy any more embarrassment."

"But it wouldn't be hilarious if they wrote about how Elizabeth rained over us longer than any other monarch? It reminds me of a poem from my boyhood about Rex the Pedigreed Piddling Pup."

Hazel chuckled but Four-eyed Tom was looking at us in such a way that I knew we had just left him several kilometres behind. When we get on a roll on topics like this, Hazel and I can entertain ourselves for hours.

"By the way, Tom, it's pronounced *kill-oh-metres*, not *kilawmuhturs*."

"I can't concentrate on my novel," he said and replaced his exercise book with a newish crossword puzzle book, slamming his concentration door on our presence. "I'm gonna work on it later."

"And it's *going to*, not *gonna* or *gunna*," Hazel told him, but we don't think he was listening.

"Heard that again last night on two different networks," I said, picking up on Hazel's admonishment to Tom. "One of the announcers was a man, the other a woman. I wondered if there were regional or gender differences in pronunciation. The woman said *gunna* and the man said *gonna*."

"God, I hate it when I hear announcers talk like that," Hazel said.

Hazel started paying attention to "that" when I went off on a rant about how crude and unprofessional those words sound when coming from the beautifully make-up-sculpted lips of certain female anchors on the networks. It was a few years ago and she's been alert to it ever since. Hazel does her own personal lip sculpting and is a quite remarkable artist.

"We're gunna come right back after these messages," Hazel said. "We're gonna go now to our Parliamentary Bureau where so and so tells us the Government is gunna ... whatever."

"You'd make a great anchor, Hazel," I told her. "You could be one of the gunna girls." I began calling one anchor on Newsworld "the gunna girl" after I heard her use that term so many times my hair caught fire.

"But first I'd have to go back to elementary school and unlearn everything."

"Or get a journalism degree," I said, "which amounts to the same thing."

Four-eyed looked up from his crossword puzzle book and said, "I've never heard of any Pedigreed Piddling Pup named Rex."

Hazel rolled her eyes and went back to her personal portable video game at the bar and left me to explain.

"It was an epic, Tom. So epic I can't remember it. I can recite almost word for word Abdul Abulbul Amir but not the one about Rex. But I do recall the whole town got concerned when he piddled through the grocery store so they sent him off to a vet for examination. Turns out Rex had diabetes."

"Arnold has been having even more accidents lately," Tom said with some concern. "Maybe I should take him on up to the vet in Medicine Hat."

When a Man Loves
(becoming) a Woman

It was after Christmas and before New Year's Eve when the members assembled to debrief on what everybody got and gave for Christmas. It is a tradition almost as old as, well, probably several years at least.

We would have done it earlier, like on Boxing Day, but Hazel refuses to open on that day. It would be perilous to knock on her door to ask if she'd open The Just One More Saloon for just one more meeting of MOOCH (Manyberries Official Officers Cocktail Hour).

The reason given for this meeting is that members want to discuss how pleasant their respective Christmas gatherings were but that's at variance with the truth. The fact is that by the 27th of December, the honourable members are going stir crazy and longing for the dim lights of the most popular nightclub in downtown Manyberries.

Purvis had arrived first and, in his haste to escape a house full of the progeny of his sons, had forgotten to change from his carpet slippers into his cowboy boots. Big Tim and I arrived minutes later, followed closely by Perley and then Four-eyed Tom, both with the look of men who had just emerged from years of solitary life in the wilderness. It should be understood that we hadn't been anywhere near The Just One More since December 24th and that sort of deprivation can wreak havoc on men's minds and souls.

The other reason we didn't really need to debrief on how pleasant our Christmas observances had been was we already knew. We had all visited each other after gift unwrapping and before turkey in a wassailing tradition that requires each host pour each guest one large mug of ouefnog laced with the rum Santa didn't drink to wash down the cookies. In keeping with his tradition, Four-eyed Tom did not have any ouefnog so, at his place, we had to content ourselves with large mugs of rum. There are some Christmas Days when we arrive home to discover that doubles of everything, including turkeys, have been laid out for the feast.

I had been up early, pacing, whiling away the hours until Hazel opened the doors by reading news on the internet and catching up with what the political pundits had been writing over the previous days. I don't know how many columns I read about Stephen Harper's serial Senate appointments and not one mention of whether there were other individuals more deserving of the sinecure.

That was my chosen topic for the agenda after we got through the niceties of the Christmas Day debrief, which generally takes no more than a minute, two at most.

But Four-eyed Tom, bless whatever soul he might possess, had arrived with a suggestion, the first time in anyone's living memory, and actually seemed prepared to participate in the conversation.

With a flourish he put a news story on the table that had come off the internet through Canoe CNEWS about a transsexual inmate serving time in a men's prison in Quebec. Tom said Tim had left it at his place when we wassailed by there on the 25th. Tom does not own a computer and has sworn he never will.

The story was about Tania, formerly known as Sylvain, who was "in transition". While recognized by Quebec authorities as a woman, the federal government disagreed, saying she was still a man.

Here, I thought, reflecting my earlier musings about political pundits focusing on the trivial, was a story with meat. This is just the sort of federal-provincial relations morass that has plagued our nation for so long and that continues to threaten the very existence of Canada as we know it. Little issues like transfer payments, offshore oil revenues, and whether three-party coalitions are good or bad suck up all the available ink and oxygen in Canada in the media's endless pursuit of trivia.

Tania was sent to the Tanguay women's prison in Montreal but there was great tension there among the women inmates because Tania was still adorned with important remnants of Sylvain. That was all the proof Corrections Canada needed to conclude that he was not yet Tania, so they sent him packing over to a men's facility in Sainte-Anne-des-Plaines. Now I know why some women insist on saying herstory, except in this case it would be more accurate to say hisherstory. Or perhaps hershistory.

I have no doubt that in the next coming-far-too-soon election, it will be Prime Minister Harper and Liberal leader Michael Ignatieff (if he's still visiting), with Quebec Premier Jean Charest chiming in, arguing over who can tell a man from a woman. They'll be trundling back and forth between Tanguay and Sainte-Anne-des-Plaines with medical experts and the media in tow trying to prove which one knows a real woman when he sees one. Any astute observer, and I stress *astute,* would see right off that this was yet another issue that could create yet another crack in Quebec/Canada relations.

"Well, seems to me," Perley said, "if he's still got the man stuff, then he's a he and a men's prison is the place for him."

Purvis agreed with Perley and said that even if his tractor ran on only three of four cylinders and the tires needed inflating it would still be a tractor.

I wondered how it was that the women in the Tanguay prison discovered that Tania was really still Sylvain. Hazel suggested that perhaps he was a little absent-minded during a lavatory break.

Then I wondered why the female inmates would be unsettled and Tom pointed out that every time Sylvain went to the shower or changed clothes all the other inmates had to remain in their cells. I wondered if maybe it wasn't the lockdown as much as curiosity that made them restless.

Tim said with the waiting lists for operating rooms as long as they are across Canada it could be years before Sylvain can find a prison that Tania could call home. I thought that's where Jack Layton would jump into the fray, especially if there were cameras and microphones present, saying that Tommy Douglas would be rolling in his grave over this health meltdown. An NDP Government would never allow a situation where a man couldn't become a woman on demand.

A lawyer representing the "still in transition" prisoner said the federal pen in which he is presently incarcerated caters specifically to men and that it's a rough institution. It occurred to me that the writer of the story might have found a better word than "caters" because a lot of Canadians still harbour the old-fashioned notion that prisons aren't there to "cater" to the inmates.

Gilles Duceppe would no doubt argue that it was all the fault of Ottawa and yet another humiliation of Quebecers, especially those waiting impatiently in line to become women.

Back at the women's prison it was reported that the woman Tania shared a cell with didn't complain, until she discovered that Tania was still Sylvain, at which point tensions started to rise. That was probably all that did, but still it was probably unnerving for the unsuspecting inmate to go to sleep worrying if she'd awake intact.

I suggested one of the parties could solve the crisis by giving inmates private rooms. But if they insisted on monogrammed towels, they'd have to do their own needlework.

Tom had given the story a lot of thought during his own incarceration between Christmas Eve and noon on the 27th. He said Sylvain should remain in the men's prison until his transition was complete and then transfer back to the women's facility. "If you give a stallion a sex change operation, it won't be a filly or a mare but it won't be jumping any fences either," he said.

We're not sure what Tom meant, we never are, but it seemed to me that the level of common sense you can find on any given day in Manyberries would be illuminating for those pundits who can't think of anything to write about except Senate appointments.

That Was No Kidney Stone – It Was a Flying Chicken

"Bert says they've taken to throwing chickens at each other in Saskatchewan," Purvis told me as I inched my chair a little closer to the table to reduce the stretching distance.

Bert and Purvis are brothers and they keep in constant touch. Bert calls when something happens in Saskatchewan, which is not often, because he has to tell somebody. Purvis calls Bert whenever he hears or reads something that proves once again, to his satisfaction, that the New Democrats are not, and never will be, ready for prime time. And whenever a Calgary newspaper reaches us that has anything in it about Calgary City Council, Purvis is on the phone calling Regina to go into his patented NDP rant. Purvis has concluded that only a New Democratic Party City Council would spend $50 million on two pedestrian bridges.

"Well, in Newfoundland, they're passing babies that they thought were kidney stones," I replied.

"What else can you do for fun in those places?" Perley asked and waved at Hazel, who was watching the final minutes of The Young and the Restless.

"What the hell are you guys talking about?" Big Tim Little asked. "Or were you over at Four-eyed Tom's sampling that new batch he just ran off?"

January, for the delegates to the Manyberries Official Officers Cocktail Hour, is weird news month. So are a lot of other months, especially the months when Parliament and various provincial legislatures are in session. But in January we try to focus on non-political weird news because, as we understand it, most Canadian politicians are away on fact-finding missions in places like Phoenix, Arizona or Clearwater Beach, Florida.

"Bert says some young guy in Tisdale was detained for throwing three live chickens into a couple of stores. He threw one into a convenience store where they sell cooked chicken to go and two more at a gas station. He was apparently yelling something about 'chicken is murder' but Bert says nobody knows what he meant."

"Could be in his excitement he mangled his phrase and meant murder is chicken," Tim said, "but even then I doubt that anybody would know what was on his mind."

"Well, he won't be going to jail or anything because he's into some sort of alternative measures program, whatever the hell that means."

Perley wondered what happened to the chickens and then told us about his grandmother who'd take an axe to their chickens every November, sparing only enough to keep them in eggs for the winter. "Man, she could lop off chicken heads, boil the feathers off and have them cleaned and ready for canning faster than two men. I always slept with one eye open when we had to go over there to visit."

Tim hauled out a story he'd taken off the Canoe website about three convicts in Vermont who were suing ConAgra Foods over some frozen chicken they purchased at the prison commissary and microwaved. One of the cons said it contained all sorts of awful things, like corn and grain. He claimed he got diarrhoea for a week, lost weight and hadn't been able to eat chicken since. He claimed further that his revulsion led to harassment by other inmates and the fact that he visited the prison infirmary with flu symptoms two days previous had nothing to do with the chicken.

The other two said they didn't get sick but suffered sympathetic emotional distress and wanted their share of the $100,000 in damages. They had even brought along evidence: the remains of the uneaten but still highly suspect chicken. The judge refused to admit it as evidence on the basis it had probably been handled by others during the three years it had been kept in storage awaiting trial.

"I was just wondering," Tim said, "if perhaps Corrections Canada had taken over the administration of the American prison system?"

"As scary as she was, my grandma still made the best canned chicken I ever ate," Perley said.

"What was that about people passing kidney stones instead of babies?" Hazel asked.

News reports out of Newfoundland, Port de Grave to be precise, told of a woman who left a New Year's Eve party to rush to hospital in Carbonear because she was suffering acute kidney stone pain. X-rays revealed that what she was passing was actually a baby. She apparently told the attending physician they'd mixed up the X-rays and that it was some other woman who was having the New Year's baby and that she was having kidney stones.

"I've heard that men only know what childbirth is like for women when they have kidney stones," Hazel said. "Anybody here ever have kidney stones?" I raised my hand.

"Was it painful?"

"Do you remember that old Marty Robbins song 'Lord You Gave Me a Mountain This Time'? At the time I was thinking Mount Everest."

"How could she not know that maybe it was time for the baby to be born?" Four-eyed Tom wondered. "I don't know anything about babies or kidney stones, but you'd think if she was expecting she might have suspected she was having her baby."

"Well, she told the media she didn't have the words to explain it so I guess that means she didn't know she was pregnant."

"I've never been to Newfoundland," Tom said and returned to his crossword puzzle.

"I owe you an apology then, Tom," I said. "I just naturally made that assumption after learning that women there give birth to kidney stones."

Who Threw the Switch?

"You know, I can't believe how dumb people are becoming," Perley told me as I sat down to join him, Purvis, Big Tim and Four-eyed Tom.

"I hope you're not talking about anybody or everybody at this table," I said.

"No, it's all Canadians, or at least over a thousand of them," Perley said. "I mean the ones who got surveyed."

"It seems somebody flipped the dimmer switch on the dimbulbs," Tim said, slipping a couple of news stories across to me to bring me up to speed. They were about surveys done for the Dominion Institute by Ipsos Reid on how knowledgeable Canadians are about our system of government. The first found that about 4 million Canadians don't even know who our Prime Minister is and 62 percent couldn't name all four parties in the House of Commons. Nearly 60 percent couldn't get past the first two lines of the National Anthem.

"The point I was making," Tim said, "is that we're churning out political illiterates from our schools and universities and telling them to go manage the future of the country. There won't be a future if the ignoramuses don't know how the country is run."

"I bet most of them know more about American politics than they do about how we do things up here," Purvis observed. "I'm pretty sure even I knew the Queen is head of state before Tim said it and even if I didn't I should have."

The 2008 survey found that 75 percent of those surveyed believed the Prime Minister or Governor General was head of state. Canadian Press reported that only 24 percent knew the answer to that question. I assumed the missing one percent had no opinion or refused to answer on the grounds that they've always wanted to say "no comment."

"They oughta make them stand up in school and say the pledge of allegiance," Four-eyed Tom offered. I told him I agreed with him, and added that in a few years they'd be ready to toddle off to Iraq to save the world.

"The bulbs are getting dimmer and dimmer by the year, no doubt about that" Perley said. "I blame the school system from grade one on up through university."

Tim said that Perley could be right and he'd personally be very reluctant to ask those same questions of his adult kids, all of whom were university graduates, for fear of how they'd respond. "I'd hate to think we raised a passel of nitwits," he confessed.

"But these were multiple choice, by the looks of it and maybe the respondents weren't paying strict attention," I argued. I figured if somebody called me at an inopportune time and asked me if our system of government is a co-operative assembly, a representative republic or a constitutional monarchy, I could be on the phone for hours arguing that it could be any one of them, depending on the day. I remember once when all parties in Parliament voted unanimously for something and they certainly looked like an assembly that was co-operating that day.

I would have answered *no* to the "representative republic" option because I don't know what that means and it sounds kind of foreign and un-Canadian. But, given the power centralized in the Prime Minister's Office, a representative republic isn't an entirely alien concept, so on certain days I might have said yes.

I might have picked "constitutional monarchy" if I wasn't asked the question on a day when I was thinking about how everything has always flowed through the PMO for a quick massage, a little lipstick and final approval.

"Anyway," I said, "I wouldn't blame the teachers' unions or even the school systems. It's the bloody-minded provinces that want the kids to grow up believing that everything worthwhile in life comes from their provincial government. They're the ones who set or approve the curriculum."

"I blame the media too," Tim said. "They should be just as obligated to educate as they are to running stories about Britney Spears' underwear, or lack of it."

"According to the survey, Quebecers are the dumbest,"," Purvis remarked. "Just read what it says: 'Half of Canadians believe they elect the prime minister directly, but in Quebec the figure was 70 percent.'"

"It's probably not their fault if they believe they're the ones who elect the prime minister," replied Big Tim. "But I guess Liberals are in the same boat if they believe they elect their party leader after the way Ignatieff got the job." The survey said that up until Ignatieff became leader, close to 100 percent of Liberal Party members believed *they* elected the guy they wanted to be prime minister.

I told my fellow Constitutional scholars of a time when I worked for CJOH television in Ottawa and was running contests to boost our daytime ratings. One woman's name was pulled for half a station wagon full of non-perishable grocery store items but she had to answer a skill-testing question first. It was during the reign of Trudeau and to make it easy I asked her to name the Prime Minister of Canada. She didn't know and said it was because she had been down with the flu for a week. I figured anybody that dense needed all the help she could get and told her to come to the studio to fetch her prize, which in the early 1970s was worth around $300.

"Maybe she had a lot of kids and then they all had a lot of kids," Tim said. "If they spread out across Canada and kept breeding, that would explain the dumbness creeping across the land."

"It might even help explain why daytime television draws such huge viewer numbers," I suggested.

Blame it on the National Energy Pogrom

Big Tim Little was bent over a writing pad and Four-eyed Tom was reading a newspaper clipping when I walked in for the Thursday official cocktail hour. Tim was working on an editorial for the Bald Prairie Rattlers Hunting & Fishing Club newsletter, The Tattler. Four-eyed Tom said it was going to be all about the National Energy Program, the legislation that was brought in by then Prime Minister Pierre Trudeau and which will never, ever, be forgotten by any Albertan, living, dead or not yet born.

"I'm not sure that revisiting the NEP will excite the readers," I said, "considering that it's revisited nearly every day in the media somewhere in Alberta, or by whoever the current Premier is at that particular moment."

"Well, we've got a whole new crisis we can blame on it," Tim said, "and like Stelmach, Klein and whatshisname, ummm, uh, Getty all said, as Albertans we are duty bound to, I forgot to mention Lougheed, remind ourselves that Ottawa exists solely to destroy Alberta."

I told Tim that our founding editor, Harry Charles, had written a similar piece wherein he reported that Purvis first experienced the agony of gout within days of Trudeau announcing the NEP. I also reminded Four-eyed Tom that he has always claimed it was no coincidence that his ancient flatbed truck started rusting during the onslaught of that particular apocalypse. Perley still wonders why it was the two rear tires on his old Pontiac station wagon went flat and his wife's raspberry patch withered all in the same year Trudeau decided that Alberta's energy wealth should be shared with other Canadians. By other Canadians, Trudeau meant his Liberal Government in

Ottawa, which would then redistribute that wealth where it was needed, that is, to areas that were suffering from critical shortages of Liberal voters.

"This is about why we pay more for food than other Canadians," Tom told me.

"I figure the academics at the University of Calgary will read this editorial and start another comprehensive study of how the NEP continues to rain down ruination on the provincial economy," Tim said. "They're into their third generation of building careers around studying the impact of Trudeau's scorched Alberta earth policies."

Tim slid the clipping across to me. It was from the Calgary Herald and had a chart showing how the prices Calgarians pay for groceries compared to national average prices. It said a Calgarian pays $7.99 for a kilogram of brown rice while the national average price is a mere $4.99. Up there in Calgary they were paying $8.99 for a kilogram of lean ground beef while other Canadians were only paying $7.18. That latter comparison wouldn't mean a whole lot to Manyberrians because we mostly eat wild game except when we can get our hands on Hutterite sausage. But it still offends us to learn that, in the heart of cattle country, we're paying more for a part of an Alberta steer than somebody in Toronto pays for exactly that same part over on the other side of that same steer.

"It's what Trudeau did," Four-eyed said, "just like he made sure they paid less for gasoline in Toronto than we pay out here, where the stuff comes from." To the best of my knowledge that was an Alberta urban myth even during the Trudeau years, but I knew that getting into a discussion with Tom over facts and figures would bog down the whole discussion.

"And we pay $5.80 more for a bunch of brown rice than they do in Ontario," he continued, thereby discrediting my conversational strategy. "And this guy Barrie only pays $2.00 for whole-wheat pasta while we're paying $6.78."

"Actually, Tom, that's not a guy named Barrie, that's a city. Barrie, Ontario is what the paper's talking about." I think at that point Tim was thinking that if Four-eyed was what you call the average reader and Purvis and Perley had yet to arrive, he might have to lower the standards of his editorial.

"So, how's your exercise in irony and sarcasm coming along?" Hazel asked as she began offloading and reloading the table.

"Tom's got me thinking I might have to make it easier for the academics in Calgary to understand," Tim said. "I'll use two different people living in two different parts of the country and compare what they pay for various food items. For instance, this guy Barrie in

Ontario pays less than a third of what Tom pays here in Manyberries for brown rice."

"That'd be wrong, Tim," Four-eyed told him. "For starters, we don't have a store in Manyberries and I have to drive up to Medicine Hat to get my groceries and that costs me a lot more for gas plus what I lose in the VLT machines. On top of that, I don't eat rice, no matter what colour it is. And who cares what Barrie pays?"

Tim looked at Tom, then at me, and then up at Hazel, and sighed. "Maybe I'll come up with something about the prospects for pheasant hunters next October."

"Or, if you want to excite the academics at the University of Calgary, you could blame the economic meltdown on the NEP," Hazel suggested.

"Geez, I like that," he said, "the roots of the Trudeau tree have strangled the world's economy."

Barracking Obama

Hazel informed us that January 20th, 2009 was going to be American History Day at The Just One More Saloon of the Southern Ranchmen's Inn in Manyberries, Alberta. And, she told us, the doors would open early so we could watch the inauguration of Barack Obama from beginning to end.

There were caveats, and the first was bar service would not commence until the legal hour. So if anybody wanted anything more than water, we would have to rent a room and go there during commercial breaks. The second was there would be no switching from American network coverage of the event to any Canadian networks.

"I want to watch *their* coverage of *their* history," she said. "And not watch what I know is going to be a bunch of drooling, probably to the point of slobbering, Canadian media types pretending or wishing that this was *our* historic event."

She announced this as we were wrapping up the previous session of the Political Official Officers Cocktail Hour, during which we spent the whole afternoon debating the merits of announcing a world class infrastructure project. Having watched the provincial, very provincial, Premiers and Prime Minister in emergency discussions about the need to get shovels into the ground, we concluded they were small thinkers. Purvis wondered why anybody would think shovels when you can use bulldozers, like the one his sons have at the ranch. "And you can charge the government rent on the dozer and bill for the operator as well," he said. "And you stick another 50 or 60 percent on top of that for handling expenses."

After five hours we still hadn't agreed on what the project might be and therefore required more discussion. We called for just one more round and that was when she said the following Tuesday would be Barack Obama's American History Day.

Big Tim Little agreed with Hazel about fawning Canadian media coverage of Obama and said he'd been watching network coverage over the last few days and the coverage was more envious than illuminating. "It won't surprise me either," he said, "if some Canadian anchor slips and refers to him as *our* new president."

"Anyway," Hazel said, "we're going to watch foreign coverage of a foreign country's historic day. I don't want you guys," and she nodded at Four-eyed Tom, "getting confused about your citizenship." Tom, being focused on either his crossword puzzle or his mystery novel about missing feet, didn't notice.

"Yeah, on the radio this morning, the guy who talks the news never once mentioned that Barack Obama was *American* President-elect," Perley said. "As if the guy were *our* President-elect."

"They probably think it's redundant to do that," I explained. "But you've got a point. People from other countries might think they're listening to American radio."

"I still don't know why they keep calling him an African-American," Four-eyed said without looking up. "I mean if the guy didn't come from Africa, why do they have to call him an African?" I noted that Tom asked the same question almost word for word as he did when we discussed the situation back during the U.S. election. I myself found it interesting that the Americans are as fond of hyphenating their citizens as Canadians are.

"A ski hill," Purvis said. "If we announce we're building a ski hill that will drag Americans up here from Montana, I bet we could get a bundle out of Ottawa."

"I'll make sure it's on the agenda after we do the debrief on the Obama inauguration," Tim told him. "That will take at least four days so the earliest we can get to it is the Monday following."

"So when will we have a day when I can read the first chapter of The Mystery of The Missing Feet?" Four-eyed Tom asked, again without looking up.

"The day following his second inauguration," Hazel said and began loading her tray with empties.

The January 20th Inappreciation of Obama

We arrived, as per Hazel's instructions, at 8:00 am MST on January 20th, 2009 to witness the inauguration of Barack Obama, the first black man in history to be elected etc. etc. etc.

Because it wasn't legal opening time, we were armed with the necessities of life of our own choosing. We had by previous arrangement chipped in and rented a ground floor room to which we could retire from the bar should the need arise. That need would arise only if we were raided by heavily armed Royal Canadian Mounted Police looking for people drinking alcohol before legal opening time in government licensed establishments. We think the likelihood of that happening has increased tenfold since the Stelmach government issued a decree forbidding Albertans to be happy during certain specified hours in places that sell liquor.

I had brought along two bottles of a very recent and inexpensive red wine and a still-sealed bottle of Tullamore Dew which my son had given me as a souvenir of a trip he took to Ireland several years earlier. I brought the Irish whiskey along to toast Mr. Obama's heritage. We had connived to convince Four-eyed Tom that Obama was really O'Bama, a fine old Irish name like O'Leary and O'Toole.

Big Tim Little, Purvis and Perley all brought six packs, and Four-eyed a mickey of the cheapest whiskey he could distil. Hazel had a thermos of green tea.

I was also armed with a note pad and three sharp pencils and explained to the other members of the Manyberries Election Official Officers Obama Watch that I was going to take notes and write an analysis of the speech for the Bald Prairie Tattler. The editor-in-chief swore it would be printed over his dead body and Big Tim Little is a relatively young man.

We were very impressed watching all the former presidents of that strange and foreign land march in and out of the White House, and agreed that whoever planned the event with such precision deserved some sort of medal. Hazel said she hadn't seen a group of people arrive with such promptitude since the five of us had arrived the day previous for the Official Cocktail Hour.

We agreed that being President of the United States of Americans must prematurely age a man. There not having been any women Presidents we were unable to guess what it might do to one of them. Hazel said, rather cattily we thought, that being the wife of Mr. President Bill hadn't been an eight year dip in the fountain of youth for Hillary. Then, even more cattily, she added that Hillary probably would have looked like The Wreck of the Hesperus if she and Bill had won the joint presidency as they had hoped before Barack came along and shattered their one last shared dream.

The whole saloon became as quiet as Grant's tomb when Obama rose to address the nation in the first inaugural speech in American history to be delivered by the first ever African-American etc. etc. etc. We were grateful that the American networks would take the time to remind us of that every 15 to 20 seconds. Hazel said she shuddered to imagine what we might be subjected to if she hadn't banned all Canadian network coverage for the day.

At about 10 paragraphs into the speech, Tim leaned over and in a whisper so as not to disturb the others' concentration, asked if I had jotted down what Barack had just said. I whispered yes. Tim looked at me and shook his head and whispered that Obama's honeymoon with Canada, and probably the Americans, wasn't going to last even 12 months. He took the pad and pencil and wrote *it must be earned.*

I missed several of the paragraphs that followed because I was wrestling with the seal on my bottle of Tullamore Dew and then had to fetch some water which I would use to prolong the pleasure of the contents.

When I returned, President Obama was waxing lyrical on *leaders and parties that cling to power through corruption and deceit and the silencing of dissent* and Tim was scribbling furiously in my note pad with one of my pencils. I didn't take umbrage because this is a fairly common practice among seasoned and professional journalists. While they don't always take notes for each other they do discuss at length precisely what angle to take on any given story so that news consumers won't get confused by reading a whole lot of differing opinions or analyses. *The Liberals in Canada are going to hate this guy in a very short time*, Tim had written. I regained control of the notebook and noted that I could actually read Tim's handwriting while my own had started out clearly but had become illegible just after where I had written *prefer leisure over work ... prefer... pleasure, fame, fortune* and after that pretty much a scrawl. At that time, I thought Barack Obama was my kind of guy because he had, in a few brief but very eloquent words, described my philosophy. I slipped the notebook and pencils back to Tim.

After it was all over and the media multitudes had been quieted, and peace and harmony had descended on the United States and The Just One More Saloon, Tim told us his theory. He said it wouldn't be long before the Liberals and New Democrats and the vast majority of Canadians fell out of love with Barack Obama. "The guy's a conservative Democrat," Tim told us. "Probably more conservative than George Bush but with a clearer understanding of what it means to be one."

"Oh, I don't know about that, Tim," I said. "I think a lot of Americans and even Canadians would dispute that."

"Did you guys follow the primaries and hear or read some of the speeches Obama made or what he said in interviews?" he asked. Hazel nodded yes.

I said, "Well of cour...well, actually, no." Perley and Purvis nodded their agreement with me and Four-eyed Tom hadn't looked up from his crossword puzzle book since he had arrived that morning.

"I'm sure that more than once he talked about people having to earn their way, much like what he said in that speech today. To put it in Canadian terms that even New Democrats and Liberals can understand, I think what he is saying is that nobody is entitled to any entitlements and if they want something they should do honest work for honest wages to buy it."

"So how would that differ from George Bush, returnee to Texas?" Hazel asked.

"Bush believed that the rich were entitled to more from their government than the poor, while Obama comes across, to me anyway, as saying *nobody* is entitled to anything unless they earn it. That's a clearer understanding of conservatism than Bush had."

"If you're correct, Tim," I said, "then he and Stephen will hit it off like soul mates. Because I think our guy has that chiselled into his psyche."

"You know what I think?" Four-eyed Tom asked. To be polite, we had to ask, not that we really wanted to know because that can be very scary sometimes.

"I think that as part of the celebration, Hazel should serve free hot dogs today because that's what Americans eat on their big holidays."

Surprisingly, Hazel agreed and said she had a wiener that had been in the freezer since the previous July 4th and Tom was welcome to it, if he immediately took it home to cook.

Robbie Burns Big Tim Little

We were in the post-New Year's Eve doldrums and it had been so unrelentingly cold that none of us had lowered our shoulders below ear level for weeks. We'd been hunched for so long that we were afraid we were beginning to look like clones of Quasimodo. We needed something to lift our spirits and Big Tim Little had an idea: a Manyberries Robbie Burns Birthday Party at The Just One More Saloon of the Southern Ranchmen's Inn for January 25.

"What, we'll gather here on a Sunday when Hazel is closed and drink scotch and recite some Scottish doggerel?" I asked. "And sing the praises of a fornicator, philanderer, tosspot and poet? Not that I don't admire and embrace those attributes."

"And eat haggis," he said, "and neeps and tatties, and listen to pipe music."

"But Tim," I said, "Hazel doesn't open Sundays, won't open Sunday night, there's probably not a piper within six hours of here and where the hell are you going to find haggis?"

Hazel came over and put down a carafe and St. Andrew's teacup and asked me if I would be coming to the Robbie Burns party. I didn't see any point in questioning Hazel's new opening hours policy, so with great pleasure I confirmed I would be in attendance.

"I'll make the haggis myself," Tim said. "You haven't eaten haggis until you've tried mine. I'll leave it in Hazel's kitchen to keep warm until we pipe it in for serving."

So it came to pass that we gathered in The Just One More on another bitter cold evening, all of us bearing the necessities for a celebration of the life and works of the Ayrshire laddie.

Everyone pitched in. Hazel dragged down an old 3 speed record player from her attic which had been a treasured possession in her teen years. While she was looking for her record player she found an even older plaid ankle-length skirt that she swore she'd never worn but that Tim said would make a perfect kilt. Perley rooted around somewhere and found a giant old 78 rpm record labelled March Past, which he said would be ideal for the occasion.

Tim had explained to Four-eyed Tom what a haggis was, and when he arrived for the celebration, Four-eyed was carrying a half gallon jug of no-name ketchup. Purvis, being worldlier, had brought along a bottle of HP Sauce. Perley and I brought bottles of other condiments from Scotland named after a famous upland bird we hunt from time to time.

Tim said he had read that a bunch of wannabe toffs in Toronto were having a Burns Night at the top of the CN Tower, Toronto's pride and glory which can be seen for miles some days when it isn't smoggy. "Ours will be better," he said, "because Robbie would prefer a ground level celebration where you don't have to crawl down hundreds of flights before you start the long crawl home."

Tim looked resplendent in the plaid skirt with his hunting boots on and his skinning knife tucked down inside the right boot. I wore plaid trousers that had been purchased many years before as a lark to wear to a charity golf tournament. I didn't wear them to the tournament because a friend said they made me look like a Scottish pimp. They still had the price tag dangling.

Hazel wore a faded plaid tam o' shanter which made her even more fetching. The other three said they'd wear their Scottishness inside with the help of the Famous Grouse.

When the time came to bring in the haggis, Perley turned the record player on. The first minute was almost total silence, allowing Tim to fetch the warm and reekin' pile from the kitchen. He waited at the door until the volume from the record player grew stronger and stronger as a gaggle of pipers marched past the microphone. With perfect timing, he walked slowly to our table and set the platter down just as the pipes reached their shrieking crescendo.

Tim reached down and yanked his hunting knife from his boot. Using both hands, he held the knife high above the haggis, and then plunged it into the steaming pudding. "An enchanting hurdie," I told Tim. "A work of art, unequalled anywhere, that pales only in comparison to those of Hazel." We were proud there was nothing dainty about him, the way we figured the Toronto tower guys would be. As we contemplated the culinary pleasures that awaited us the sound of the pipes began to fade, softening in a gentle diminuendo into silence.

Tim insisted that Purvis and Four-eyed Tom had to sample a small bit before they adorned their share with the ketchup or HP Sauce.

They did and Purvis decided it wasn't as bad as he remembered and left his HP in the bottle. Four-eyed Tom drowned his portion because, as he said, it needed a little moistening.

The neeps and tatties were in separate bowls, each topped by a half brick of butter sided by two smaller bowls of coarsely ground peppercorns which Tim said was probably the way the Scots would have served pepper back in those days, if they had any pepper.

I made the first toast:

> And here's to the Noble Big Tim Little
> Renowned for the art he creates on the griddle

Hazel made the second one:

> Here's to he who gets too wordy
> But I like it when he flatters my hurdies

A few more sips of guid ol' whisky and I recalled a few more lines of Burns and told Hazel that she had a *beauty more murderously fatal than a stiletto or poisoned arrow.*

If you had been in Manyberries that night when the thermometer hit minus 30 C with a wind-chill of minus 40, you might have been drawn to the one window where you could see light and peeked inside. That would have been the window of The Just One More Saloon of the Southern Ranchmen's Inn. You would have seen six people sitting together, close, snug and warm, eating haggis and neeps & tatties, and toasting each other. And if you knew it was Robbie Burns Day, and if you knew anything about the real Robbie Burns, you would know that what you were seeing through that window was how – and where – Robbie himself would have celebrated his birthday if he were still with us.

The Booby Prize

"Sweet suffering mother, I don't know what the world of women is coming to," Hazel said. "They must have gone crazy down there, I mean down east. In what I think they call the Greater Toronto Area."

"Well, I'm relieved that it's not men who are getting your dander up, although it's still fairly early in the day," I replied."

"Did you read about it, this woman who was told she couldn't breast feed her baby in a pool that is owned by a private company but open to the public?"

"No, can't recall anything like that," I replied. "But I can see problems with breast feeding a baby in a swimming pool if the kid hasn't learned how to snorkel."

Hazel laughed and Four-eyed Tom got up and walked over to his other table in the dark corner. There are some men, I guess, who just aren't comfortable discussing the intricacies of breast feeding a child while doing laps in a pool.

"Actually, the woman was sitting in the pool nursing the kid and the owner asked her to move to the change room or the viewing gallery to continue. Apparently provincial regulations forbid food and drink in public pool areas."

"Makes sense to me. In Palm Springs they forbid glass bottles and glasses, even around the private condo pools. The retirees have to put their teeth in Tupperware if they don't wear them while swimming."

"Anyway, in this incident in Toronto, the pool owner was abiding by the law and well within her rights to ask the mother to move, but it didn't end there."

"It never does, not around Toronto," I said. "Those people are the worst when it comes to opportunities to run crying to the media if it relieves their pain or suffering or shame or whatever it was they experienced."

"The mother said it was the first time she suffered discrimination, wanted to cry, tried to pretend it never happened and was completely sad, lost and numb." Hazel sat down, reached across and topped up my wine glass, which meant she wanted an audience and I was it.

"Can you imagine anybody coming close to a nervous breakdown over something as trivial as that?"

"But Hazel, you have to remember people down there don't think like normal people. Ontario is the capital of tender sensitivities, political correctness, entitlement and modern thought, not to forget demanding apologies from anybody who might be suspected of having offended somebody, sometime, somewhere."

"They organized a nurse-in at the pool," Hazel said. "A peaceful nurse-in. They called in nursing mothers from all over the region to join them in protesting discrimination against breast feeding."

"So they had a bunch of bare-breasted moms nursing their babies while chanting Hell No, We Won't Go? Geez, I'm surprised the networks weren't there live on location. Not for salacious reasons of course, but for the ratings."

"If some young mom came in here and started nursing her baby, there's no way I'd tell her to move someplace more discreet. But this is private property and I'd have every right to do it. Don't they have property rights in Ontario?"

Four-eyed Tom returned for his second beer mug. "When you're finished talking about this," he said, "I'll come back."

"We'll be at this for hours, Tom," I said. He went back to the corner and I turned back to answer Hazel.

"Yes, they have some property rights but they also have these Human Rights Commissions and they appear to have more clout than Parliament and the Supreme Court combined."

"I hope it's not true that 'what you eat is what you are' because that baby is going to have a helluva time when he or she gets out into the real world," she said.

Bean Pot Danny

"So Newfoundland is thinking about declaring independence from Canada," Big Tim told me as I waved frantically at Hazel in the hope that she'd recognize a victim of dehydration.

"Yeah, I read Martin's column this morning." The online edition of the Calgary Herald had a column by Don Martin with the headline "Newfie Screech for sovereignty makes no sense."

"Strange time to be talking about separation with crude prices going south faster than the government surplus," Purvis said. "Or did Danny Williams blame that on Stephen too?"

The consensus of the members of the Manyberries Official Officers Cocktail Hour (MOOCH) is that Danny Williams has blamed Harper for everything that's gone wrong in Newfoundland since April 1st, 1949, the day Newfoundland joined Confederation. Danny isn't alone – here in Alberta we blame everything that goes wrong and that will ever go wrong on Pierre Trudeau and the National Energy Program. In fact, as of this moment, we are blaming Trudeau for the decline in crude oil prices to more realistic and therefore less profitable levels.

"I guess if they did separate Danny Williams would have himself crowned monarch," Tim said. "King Danny, the Cock of the Rock. Or maybe God of the Cod People? I think I've been in here hanging around with you guys too much."

"If Hazel would give us that red enamel sauce pan from her collection we could send him that to wear as his symbol of high office," I suggested. "He could wear it when he visits Ottawa to begin negotiations. And use it to soak and cook his beans in when he finds out that the offshore reserves belong to the feds."

Perley thought the Newfoundland separatists could call themselves the Rock Block, a variation on the Bloc Quebecois. "They could be Rockheads, like the Blocheads."

"He should read what that Swami Coomasomething guy you told me about wrote a long time ago," Purvis said, addressing me.

I had to ponder that until I realized he was talking about Ananda Coomaraswamy, a Ceylonese philosopher. He said he knew it sounded something like Swami something.

"What's that all about?" Tim wondered.

"Coomaraswamy was an academic/philosopher and I don't know what else. I read some of his stuff back when I was in high school. I had part of a collection of Great Books of the Western World that I picked up at a yard sale."

"What did he write about Newfoundland?"

"Nothing, he wrote about the wide gap between the East and West but he was talking about so-called Western Culture and the cultures of the Middle East and Far East."

"Might have some application here," Tim said. "You can't find a much bigger gap between east and west than the one we have here in Canada."

The Crash of Purvis

"Dammit, this financial crisis is depressing," Purvis moaned as he sat down. He moans every time he sits down because of his bad back but this moan had even more pain in it than usual.

"Did you get side-swiped by the meltdown, Purvis?" Perley asked and got an affirmative nod in response.

We don't know how much money is left in the world but we're certain that Purvis has most of it. He had several tonnes stashed in his RRSP before he retired and even more after he got in very early at two bits a share in a little Calgary gold mining company called Bre-X. We know all about this because at least once a week Purvis lectures us on buying low and selling high and cites his own personal experience. He has told us he very generously sold when the shares hit $125.00 so other people could make some money too.

Today, however, he had definitely lost much of his usual swagger. "My broker called me and said it was depressing as hell but that it's a better time to be buying than selling. That's what Stephen said too so I decided the time was right to pick up some bargains. But I told my broker to stay away from those big corporate endtitties that started this whole mess."

Our Prime Minister, Stephen, said that he thought there were some real buying opportunities out there when world markets crashed. I took his advice and put some change into a brewery conglomerate and pledged to never drink anything but their beer and urged everybody else to do the same. I still thought it was a good investment even after they pointed out that I only drink beer about twice a year.

"Just make sure you avoid the companies that went bankrupt," Perley said to Purvis. "I wouldn't put a dime into anything those guys were running."

"That's what I was thinking," Purvis said. "They oughta take those guys on Wall Street and horsewhip them. Geez, I'm down 40 percent and I didn't even have money in any one of their companies. But at least my distillery shares are flying high, because, as you'd expect in times like these, they're heading heavenward."

"Maybe I should have gone distillery instead of brewery," I said. "I figured the stockbrokers and high rollers would be drowning their sorrows in the cheap stuff but I guess I was wrong."

"Did you hear about the cash bonuses those guys got when their companies went belly-up or got bailed out?" Four-eyed Tom asked. "They run a company into the ground and then turn around and collect a reward for it."

"You know what it is, eh?" Purvis asked. "These guys running those big endtitties get out of touch. They spend all their time trying to figure out how to spend the money they earn and don't pay any attention to their jobs. Now I, for instance, I spend more time trying to figure out ways to make money than on how to get rid of it."

"Sort of like Hazel, right?" Perley said and gave her a wink as she began making space for round four.

"Oh yeah," she said, "I'm up all night stacking coins and entering the amounts in my tips journal. I should be able to drive to Medicine Hat in a year or two on that." Medicine Hat is a short commute north of Manyberries.

"What frosts me," Purvis said, "is nobody ever goes to jail. Nobody ever gets horsewhipped and they still get to live in their mansions and drive their fancy cars. What the hell was wrong with George Bush that he didn't go after these guys and pin their hides to the barn wall? But what can you expect from a Texan!"

It should be explained there are some Albertans who think Texans are all hat and no cattle, and Purvis is one of them. He doesn't dislike George Bush, it's just that, well, even if he is no longer president, George is still a Texan and owns a ranch down there and Purvis is very suspicious about the size of that ranch and doubts there are really enough acres to qualify as one. The media have never, to our knowledge, ever reported the total acreage and that alone is reason enough to be suspicious, according to Purvis. He once said the media will report everything about politicians including their own personal sizes but there's never been a mention of the size of George Bush's ranch. Purvis was down there one time – to Texas, that is, not to George Bush's ranch – and he says there are people sitting on 10 acre plots and calling them ranches. Around Manyberries you couldn't run one dwarf cow on 10 acres because this is short grass country. "There's a lot of goat ropers down in Texas, and for all we know Bush is one of them" he said.

I made a mental note to write to Katie Couric to suggest she might do some investigative reporting on the size of the Bush ranch. I thought I'd add that while she was at it she might want to investigate some other Bush sizes as well, like what size hat and boots he wears, and what brand. And perhaps ask him what exactly he did during those eight years.

"And now the governments are bailing out banks, businesses, stockbrokers and who knows what else, and they're using our money to do it." Purvis shook his head in disgust. "And I haven't heard anything about what they plan to do for ranchers. There are a lot of those guys who probably had shares in various outfits. What are they gonna do if the real backbone of society gets broken? What will happen if *ranchers* are driven out of business?"

"Probably give them better terms on the loans for their Cadillacs or their Lincoln Town Cars," Perley said. That seemed to satisfy Purvis.

"I read that some of those guys went off on wild weekends in private jets after they got some of that government bailout money," Four-eyed said. "And they got away with it. I always thought if we ever got a bank again in Manyberries, I'd like to work at it."

"Yeah, a wild weekend in Medicine Hat would be good for the soul," Big Tim said.

"Well, the way I figure it is these outfits got too big. Business isn't like ranching where you can never get too big." Purvis took a thoughtful swallow. "You get these New York endtitties so big they figure nothing can stop them and whatever they do is the right thing and all of a sudden, they collapse. The government should have stepped in years ago."

"You're right, Purvis," Tim said. "And maybe the worst is still to come because we haven't heard yet what's going on with the equally big entities."

"It'll probably be just more bad news when that comes out," Purvis moaned.

The Merry Wives of Manyberries

"Did you read or hear about that couple going to court to get paternity *and* maternity leave support because they were about to have twins?" Hazel had already put down the entitlements to which Perley and I were entitled by virtue of our presence and sat down in what is traditionally Four-eyed Tom's chair. It's a far less wasteful use of that space when Hazel occupies it.

"No, can't say as I did, but then Perley and I are in the middle of our three day pledge not to read or hear or watch anything but weird stuff in the news." This is the way Perley and I protest when something objectionable is carried by the media. That usually means stories out of Ottawa, Edmonton, other provincial capitals or Calgary. Even on those rare occasions when the media report just the facts without a lot of superfluous analysis we find some stories objectionable. The story that had offended us this time was that Stephen Harper appointed a mob of new Senators to fill vacancies in the upper chamber pot. It wasn't the story itself we found offensive, it was the accompanying list of who got the goodies: there was nobody from Manyberries on it.

There isn't anybody in Manyberries who would have turned turn down a Senate appointment after we read of one Senator who spent all of his time in Mexico and hardly ever went near Ottawa. It's not that we'd want to spend 12 months of the year in Mexico but when the temperature in winter hits minus 27, a few months in a foreign country learning their traditions and culture suddenly looks very attractive. And Mexico is less foreign to Manyberrians than Ottawa, which makes it even more appealing.

"Well," Hazel said, returning to her choice of topic for the agenda, "this couple argues that because they're having twins, both parents have the constitutional right to take paid leave from their jobs. Hell, I didn't even know they paid people to take time off to spend with their babies."

"The guy would have to take another wife if they had triplets," Perley said. "And what if a couple had quadruplets? Would they each get two years or would one take three and the other one year?"

"Great, a young guy with some energy and ambition and several wives could retire nine months into his multiple marriages and never have to work again," I said with a very large trace of envy. It wasn't nearly as large a trace as what I was feeling about the Senate appointments, but by anybody's measure it was still very large.

"You're not going to impress any women I know with that theory," Hazel warned me. "Not that I know any women who'd be impressed by you no matter what you said or did."

I explained I wasn't arguing for multiple wives as much as calculating the profits that might accrue. For instance, if a young guy married five wives and the first wife delivered a child nine months into the marriage, the guy qualifies for a whole year off work. With perfect timing, he could move from that first 12 months of paternity leave into another 12. If all the partners agreed to go beyond the traditional 1.3 children per married couple to, say four children per mother, he's got a 20 year stretch of no work ahead of him.

"So where would they get the money it would take to feed and house a population approaching that of Manyberries?" Hazel asked.

I hadn't thought of that because, quite frankly, I hadn't given it any thought. I'm more of a short term plan guy than what you might call a forward planner. But Perley had a solution.

He explained that if each wife took a job up until it was time to deliver the baby, then she'd be eligible for a year off with pay. "Now they've doubled their income," he said, "and if they were able to time it right, they could have two, three, maybe four incomes all at the same time."

"Well, keep working on it," Hazel said and stood to return to the bar. "If you can find a way to make it work, you can tell Stephen you're not interested in a Senate appointment."

Infralapsarian Infrastructure

The debate about getting infrastructure projects for Manyberries is always a hot topic at The Just One More Saloon. Purvis had proposed that we build a ski hill, but some of us thought that haste might make waste and we didn't want to leave future generations with something like the Olympic Oval in Montreal. Besides, a ski hill is very seasonal and, as one of us said, adding an 18 hole golf course would make it an almost year-round attraction.

Perley pointed out that at some golf courses, when they close for the season and before the snow arrives, deer are often seen grazing. If we were to open the golf course to hunters in November we could squeeze in another month of revenue. He calculated that hunters would enthusiastically rent a golf cart to go out and shoot their deer and stop off at the 9th hole canteen for a beer and hot dog before returning to the club house for more food and refreshments but only if it could be ascertained it would have no financial impact on The Just One More Saloon. That last caveat was added at the insistence of Hazel. Four-eyed Tom said he had seen geese all over a lot of courses but we rejected opening ours to hunters in October because it would conflict with the golfers getting their last whacks in before the heavy frost arrives.

There was some urgency to our discussions because rumour had it Old Rutherford and the Mrs were planning to expand the tanning bed parlour they have in their trailer using federal infrastructure money. We knew it was imperative that we come up with a project and plan that would get shovels into the ground before Old Rutherford scooped the money allocated for Manyberries.

"Even though it's a stupid idea, we're not going to behave like the Premiers and cast aspersions on Old Rutherford's project," Big Tim said. "When they go to Ottawa it's always 'my province first.' We don't want Canadians thinking we're as small-minded as they are. We'll get somebody else to call it stupid."

"Bert called me from Regina and said that a tanning parlour bed caught fire there the other day," Purvis reported. "Would we be acting like provincial Premiers if we told Stephen that tanning parlours could be harmful to future generations?"

"Not if we do it respectfully," Tim said. "We'd just make the case that a ski and golf resort development wouldn't pose a fire hazard to future generations like an ill-considered, expensive, not to forget skin-damaging tanning parlour expansion, which other people, independent observers, are calling stupid."

Four-eyed Tom was looking concerned. He is a frequent customer at Old Rutherford's tanning parlour. "Did anybody get burned in that fire?"

"No, but Bert said the young guy in the bed had a helluva time getting out of it when it caught fire. I've gotta remember to tell the wife about that. She's still spending a lot of the grocery money I give her over there in the Rutherford's trailer every week."

"What about sewers?" Four-eyed Tom asked. He had set aside his crossword puzzle book and was fully engaged because whatever the project there was a good chance he could get in on the swag with his flatbed truck (every project has at least one flatbed truck). "They were talking about infrastructure for the future, like roads and sewers and stuff."

"What would we do with our outhouses if we got sewers?" Purvis asked.

"Well, they've got that windmill museum over in Etzikom," Perley mused. "Why don't we build an outhouse museum to get some of that tourism business over here?"

"Or we could put them right there on the golf course itself, one at every hole," Tim said. "I don't know of any golf course that has a toilet for every hole. And they could double as storm shelters." Tim is a little like Zorba the Greek in that he is always willing to encourage us when we launch what will undoubtedly become known as "the whole catastrophe".

"Whatever we build, it has to be for the ages," Purvis said. "Like a ski hill. Once you've built a hill that big, it's gonna be there forever."

"So would the valley that we'd create when we dig the dirt for the hill," Perley said. "But I guess we could put some of the golf course down in the valley and scatter the rest of it around the base of the mountain."

Purvis said whatever the project, and he favoured a ski hill, it should require the work of a bulldozer and operator. His sons have one at the ranch and Purvis loves operating the thing. Perley said he'd drive his old Pontiac station wagon to ferry food and workers to and from the job site. I said if I could charge the battery on my hunting Suburban, I'd drive it as an emergency evacuation vehicle if the government sent in inspectors.

"Would they put up a monument with our names on it?" Four-eyed wondered. "You know, like they're gonna do on those billion dollar bridges those guys are going to get built up in Calgary. I'd sort of like having a monument with my name on it for people in the future to read."

"Within 20, 30 years at most, there'll be a monument somewhere with your name on it, Tom," Hazel said.

By the time the gavel slammed down on that meeting, we still hadn't decided if a ski hill and golf course would be our infrastructure project. Actually, we don't have a gavel so we rely on Hazel to signal the end of the meeting and she does that by slamming down the last round.

But we did agree that it was extremely urgent that we get some sort of project on the drawing board to help our governments nurse the economy back to health. As citizens, in times like these, we have to pull together to create jobs, boost consumer spending and leave future generations with something monumental to see for the debt they're paying. And of course, to make sure we get our hands on the money before Old Rutherford gets his greedy paws on it.

The Inhibited Left

"You're ambidextrous, right?" Hazel asked as she put my carafe and a Mickey Mouse juice glass in front of me. She is a born-again flea market shopper and when she can get away from The Just One More Saloon you'll find her scouring any and all flea markets and second hand stores within a day's drive of Manyberries.

"Depends on what ambidextrous means coming from you," I said cautiously. "If it means do I like to wear girly stuff, then no. If your question is a prelude to an invitation to experiment, then the answer is yes."

She gave me a look that was as shrivelling as a dip in a winter lake. "In your dreams, cowboy. No, I just finished an article on the internet about left-handed people being different from right-handed." She handed me a printout to read.

Some researchers had determined that left-handed people are more inhibited than their right-handed neighbours and live in fear of making mistakes.

"Actually, come to think of it, I guess you could say I'm partially ambidextrous," I said. "I write with my right hand but golf from the left, and I played baseball and hockey from the left."

"You obviously have no fear of making mistakes, which is surprising, considering your track record. Could be you're a half-and-half type."

"I was trained not to make mistakes," I told her as Purvis, Big Tim, Perley and Four-eyed Tom arrived and took up their stations.

"He stopped making mistakes when he was living in Ottawa," Perley said. "He learned if you never make a decision you never make mistakes."

"Or you sit on committees of dozens of people so nobody will ever know just where it was the buck stopped," Big Tim added.

"Are any of you guys left-handed?" Hazel asked and they all shook their heads no.

Four-eyed Tom took his crossword puzzle book out and spread it on the table, pencil gripped tightly in his left hand hovering over the page. Hazel looked at him and then at the rest of us and shook her head.

I handed the printout to Purvis, who gave it a scan, shrugged his shoulders and handed it on to Perley, who passed it on to Tim without giving it a glance.

"It says here a couple of famous left-handers from the distant and recent past include Jack the Ripper and Bill Clinton," Tim said, glancing over the printout quickly before he handed it back to Hazel. "These researchers are dead wrong in their conclusions."

"Hold that thought and I'll be right back," Hazel told him and went to the bar to get our order ready for shipping.

"Did you read about that couple over in Abbotsford who just welcomed their 18th child?" Tim asked while Hazel was gone. "That's 18 kids in 23 years of marriage – 10 girls and eight boys – and the oldest just turned 23."

"Wonder if the parents are right-handed?" I said.

"That's five foursomes, if they golf," Tim said. That'd be a thousand bucks a round minimum even if they don't use power carts."

"I don't think any mom who's had 18 kids is likely to be walking 18 holes."

Hazel returned and began offloading. "What mom had 18 kids?" she asked.

"A couple who emigrated from Romania to Abbotsford," Tim replied.

"And I thought I was busy looking after you guys. Anyway, why do you say those researchers are wrong about left-handers?"

"Would you call Bill Clinton inhibited?" Tim asked her. "Or maybe we should ask Monica Lewinsky for her thoughts on the subject."

"Or Hillary," I suggested. "She might have some insights."

"But he swore he never had sex with that woman," Hazel argued. "Monica, I mean, not Hillary."

"Well, in his own sweet hillbilly way, Clinton denied making a mistake," I said. "And will probably go to his grave insisting he did nothing to sully or leave a stain on the Office of the President. It was all Oval Office innocence. All he did was share a cigar in a place I thought would have been designated non-smoking."

"I wouldn't call Jack the Ripper inhibited either," Tim said. "And

I'm certain he never would have admitted that anything he did was a mistake."

"So you two guys," Hazel nodded at me and Tim, "don't think left-handers are more inhibited than right-handers. And you guys," she nodded at the other three, "don't care."

"I'm right-handed," Purvis said, "and I hate making mistakes that cost me money."

"I don't think about it," Four-eyed Tom said without looking up from his crossword.

"I'm like the guy who sang he doesn't care if it rains or freezes as long as he's got his plastic Jesus sitting up there on the dashboard of his truck," Perley told her.

"I'm half right and half left," I said, "and I sleep naked, so what does that mean?"

"Probably that you sleep alone," she said.

Standing Up for Autoworkers

"Do you know any retired autoworkers?" Hazel asked after she had deposited my carafe, and to my surprise a stemmed wine glass, on the table.

"I think a couple of cousins in Ontario might have worked for the industry and are no doubt retired but they wouldn't know where Manyberries is and my best guess is they moved to Florida."

"I was thinking one of them might make a good catch," she said and dropped a computer printout on the table. She went back to the bar and I picked up the paper and gave it a scan. It was about how General Motors was spending $17 million a year on Viagra and other lifestyle drugs for both unionized and salaried employees.

Hazel returned with a pickled oeuf and some bite-sized super-spiced pepperoni sticks she had thoughtfully sliced for me. She pulled a bottle of Tabasco sauce from her hip pocket and set it beside the plate. "I saw you drive out to look for pheasants this morning," she said, "and thought you probably missed lunch. Anyway, what do you think of that story?"

"Three things," I said. "First, it says health care adds $1,500 to the price of every vehicle GM sells, which is an awfully stiff expense for consumers to absorb, if you'll pardon what I didn't intend as a pun, if that's what it was. Second, at a time when GM is on the ropes you'd think the employees would want to spend all of their spare time trying to save the company. And third, I used to say that who needs Viagra when there are women around but I've refined that to who needs Viagra when you're in the presence of Hazel?"

She gave me a bump with her hip and told me flattery would get me everywhere. I hauled out my own story that I had picked up off Sympatico. It was an AP story out of London, England.

"This says," I told Hazel, "that there is a huge shortage of sperm donors in Britain. There are 4,000 women a year who need assistance and only 307 men registered to help them."

"They must be busy guys."

"But here's another," I told her, and hauled out a second AP report. This story was headlined "Grandma births own grandchildren," and was from Cleveland, Ohio. "Doesn't it seem to you like there's a whole flood of stories of this type these days?"

"Let me see that one," she said and was reading it when Big Tim Little, Four-eyed Tom, Perley and Purvis walked in to give us a quorum for the Manyberries Official Cocktail Hour.

"It says here," Hazel told them, "that a 56-year-old woman in Ohio gave birth to her triplet grandchildren for her daughter and son-in-law."

"Isn't that what causes divorces?" Tom asked.

"Used to," Purvis said, "but now that Obama is President, maybe they've changed the laws. Never would have happened if they'd elected Sarah Palin Vice-President."

"I remember an old novelty song on the radio years ago," Perley said. "It was called 'I'm my own Grandpa'. So these kids will be singing that when they grow up."

"Gives me the shivers," Hazel said. "And not the good kind."

"Well, it keeps it in the family," Big Tim said. "And there's a lot of politicians down there and just as many up here who claim to support family friendly government policies."

"I think I'd rather find a friendly retired autoworker," Hazel said and returned to the bar to get supplies for the recent arrivals.

"What's she talking about?" Purvis asked.

"Probably thinks just because I'm not a schooled mechanic that I'm not good enough to work on her vehicle," Four-eyed Tom said.

"Tom," I told him, "You are so absolutely 100 percent correct it's astounding."

A Seminal Debate

I was bent over a clipping from the Calgary Herald and Four-eyed Tom was bent over one of his crossword puzzle books when Perley and Purvis arrived for the cocktail hour. Big Tim Little had been sitting at a table over near the bar chatting with Hazel but came over to join us as P & P took their chairs.

"We've got another cross-border crisis looming, boys," I said, "and this one will make the mad cow and softwood lumber disputes look like mice up against elephants."

"Oh geez," Purvis said, "we haven't even got by the mad cow thing, not with those free trade and free enterprise ranchers down there whining about competition. What're the Americans bitching about now?"

"Our elephant sperm," I said. "The headline in the Herald says 'Canadian elephant's sperm quality sparks cross-border battle.' If they don't close the border because of terrorists, mad cows, softwood lumber and who knows what else, this just might be what slams the gates from coast to coast."

"We must be getting close to April," Perley said, "or he wouldn't be fussing over whether the border's open or closed."

"What is it about April?" Big Tim Little asked me.

"I go to Palm Springs every April to get my golf muscles in shape for summer."

"Waste of money," Purvis said "What in hell is all this about elephant sperm?"

"Well, it seems some animal rights advocates in Washington State are trying to stop a Canadian zoo from shipping elephant sperm to a zoo in Seattle. They claim it's a load of bad seed because it could be carrying a deadly elephant herpes virus."

Perley had taken the clipping from me and was scanning it. "Says here," he read, "that our elephant's name is Rex and that he's an easygoing guy and that he lives in Ontario. It says he's 39 years old and already the father of three. It says his bride to be is called Chai, who's 29 years old." He turned to me. "Chai? Isn't that the stuff you bought at that coffee joint when we were up in Calgary last month?"

"Yeah, but that was tea and I ordered regular, not the elephant size."

"You guys know there are no elephants in Canada," Four-eyed Tom informed us and bent back down over his crossword book.

"There are in zoos, Tom," Big Tim Little assured him and waved at Hazel to let her know our compound had gone dry.

"It says here that Asian elephant sperm has not been successfully used after being frozen," Perley said, "so they plan to send 'fresh chilled semen' to Seattle. Sounds like a commercial for Florida orange juice."

Now it was Big Tim Little's turn. "It says here they made one earlier stab, stab is my word, not the newspaper's, but it didn't work." Big Tim was biting his lower lip so hard I thought it might bleed. "It says what Rex sent them was of good quality and the timing was excellent and, they thought, so was a load they got from two other elephants in Oklahoma and Arizona, but nothing worked."

"Of course, we did have elephants here thousands of years ago," Four-eyed Tom said, "but they were great big hairy critters and they didn't call them elephants." He went back to his crossword book while the rest of us struggled to find the appropriate words to acknowledge his contribution.

"So what's the topic for tonight?" Hazel wondered and started filling the spaces between the empties with fullies. "Naked pogo stick races down main street?"

"Elephant semen," Purvis said, "and the anti-Canadianism of American tree-huggers."

"I'm sure you won't mind if I don't join you and leave you the key so you can lock up when you leave," she said. "In the meantime, if you want to wave at me again, move over to a clear table."

"The guy who runs the elephants at the Seattle zoo, his name is Bruce Upchurch and he's also in charge of behavioural management, says the Asian elephant population is in jeopardy," Big Tim said. "It's because of an aging population, a low birth rate and low number of fertile daddy elephants."

"Sounds like Manyberries," Hazel said.

"So, if they put Rex in a truck that takes him to Washington and they won't let him into the States, why don't they bring the lady elephant up here?" Four-eyed Tom was now fully engaged because he had closed his crossword puzzle book and placed it on an adjacent table where it wouldn't dampen from spilled beer and wine.

"They don't actually do it that way anymore, Tom," Purvis said. Purvis lived on a ranch all his life and he's an expert on complicated stuff like this. "They don't have to put the bull and cow together."

Four-eyed didn't say anything, just sat looking at Purvis waiting for him to explain what he meant.

"They ship the semen to wherever it's needed, Tom. The bull doesn't have to go with it." Big Tim Little thought he was helping ease Four-eyed's confusion. He wasn't.

"How can they send an elephant's semen all the way from Ontario to Washington?" Four-eyed took a swallow. "This sounds like a made up story."

Purvis leaped into the fray. "Tell you what, Tom. Next month you come out to the ranch with me. My sons have some bulls there that are among the best in the world. Those bulls are in demand and they have a, well, they'll be preparing a shipment for Brazil. You come with me and you'll get a clear understanding of what this elephant thing is all about."

"Should I bring anything? What will I have to do?" Tom asked.

"Just pretend," Purvis said, "that my son's bulls are elephants."

Of Gravest Concern

"Somebody was in here looking for you the other night," Perley informed me, "but we told him that you don't live here anymore."

"It was a guy who said he'd read a column you wrote for the Calgary Herald about coyotes in the city up there and he was in the neighbourhood and wanted to talk to you about it." Purvis gave Hazel a coyote howl to signal that we'd appreciate a visit if she could spare the time.

"What did you write about coyotes?" Perley asked.

"I said, in so many words, that somebody should shoot them before they attack and eat any more cats and dogs and then graduate to small children."

"You mean they don't shoot coyotes when they see them up there?" Purvis was surprised to hear that in Alberta there are people who don't automatically haul out the artillery when they spot a coyote. Around here, and in most parts of the province where people aren't too far removed from wildlife, shooting coyotes is a public service. It's not that we don't admire the sneaky way they live, coming in quietly at night to pick off our cats, dogs and newborn calves, it's just that the expense of having them around as dinner guests is considered excessive by most folks. In that respect they're like visiting politicians except that coyotes are always here; always just over the nearest hill.

"So what did the guy want – to argue, or agree with me?" I asked.

"Said he had a rifle he figured would be perfect for coyote shooters and wanted to sell it to you." Perley thanked Hazel for taking the time to come and visit our table. "You haven't been around so we figured you left town and that's what we told him."

"I told you guys in March I was going to Palm Springs," I said. "In fact, I bought you a round on March 30 before I left for the Calgary airport."

"Well, we're old, senior citizens in fact, so you can't expect us to remember everything," Perley explained.

"What's new in Palm Springs?" Purvis asked. I expect he was being polite because I don't suppose he cares about what's new, or old, in Palm Springs.

"Well, I think I spotted a business opportunity for you, Purvis," I said, and hauled out an advertisement from the Desert Sun, which is the Coachella Valley's excellent daily newspaper.

"It says here you can turn your un-needed cemetery property into cash. They'll even buy mausoleums and cremation niches in addition to graves."

"I don't own any un-needed cemetery property," Purvis said. "All I own now is a quarter section of hard scrabble prairie where you might, if you spent the time, be able to grow carrots between the rocks."

"I see where he's going with this," Perley told Purvis. "He's probably thinking you could convert your quarter into a cemetery and sell plots. If you figured every grave was six deep and three wide, that's a lot of plots in 160 acres."

"I should have brought my slide rule," Big Tim said, "and I could have told you how many. It'd run well into the multiple thousands."

"How much would they pay per plot?" Purvis asked.

I flipped the advertisement over and told them the same company was offering end-of-life insurance with no medical exams or blood tests required. "It says on this side that a non-smoking, 62-year-old male would pay only $44.10 a month and when the time came the company would pay his estate $10,000."

Purvis grabbed the advertisement to read for himself. It's not that he doesn't trust what I say but for Purvis, like too many Canadians, if it's printed in a newspaper it must be gospel.

"Cremation niches," he mused out loud. "Wonder instead if they'd accept holes in the ground?"

"You mean you'd dig a hole in the ground and put the urn in there?" Perley asked.

"No, we're Albertans and if we're going to start thinking, we should think big and that's what I'm doing here. I could go and get the power posthole augur from the ranch and drill postholes all over the quarter. I'd go down six feet, which would be deep enough to hold three urns." He took out his shirt pocket spiral notebook and stubby pencil.

"Don't strain yourself, Purvis," Big Tim told him, "I can tell you right now you'd have space on that quarter for millions of occupants."

"So if I cut a deal with the insurance company to take all their urn business for a straight $1,000, GST included, times millions and millions?"

"I don't have my calculator," I said, "but I think the millions are turning into billions."

"How will you mark the graves for when people come to visit their loved ones?" Four-eyed Tom asked. "If you're putting them in three to a hole, that's going to require a lot of head stones."

"Who's ever gonna come up here from Palm Springs?" Perley said. "Except him," jerking a thumb in my direction, "and he has to because he lives here and has to come home."

"Anyway, that's just the sort of question a bureaucrat would ask, Tom, because they don't think big." Purvis shook his head. "I would have thought it more likely that the question would have come from him," and he pointed in my direction.

"You know," he said to me, "I was thinking that all those years in Ottawa might have dulled your edge, killed your free enterprise spirit, and turned you into a bureaucrat. I was wrong and I apologize." He held up a hand and pointed down at me as a signal to Hazel I was to be rewarded.

When Hazel arrived with my glass, Purvis looked up at her and said, "That young fella over there didn't get Ottawashed after all. By jiminy the good old Alberta spirit still throbs in him as strong as ever."

"I'm relieved that something does," she said.

The Newfoundland Cardinal

"Well, we witnessed an historic event," Big Tim Little said. "Though not so historic that your grandchildren would gather round your chair to hear you tell of it."

We had been half-heartedly discussing the news that Newfoundland had become a "have" province while Ontario had slipped into "have not" status. Half-heartedly because, well, who really cares? Newfoundland and Ontario are Canadian provinces located east of Manyberries.

It has been our collective observation that, apart from a few politicians, nobody ever discusses who's a "have" and who's a "have not". On the other hand, you could spend many – more than many – cocktail hours in heated discussion on the status of Manyberries in that regard. Despite our enviable advantages and blessings, it is our official position when dealing with both federal and provincial governments that we are the official "have not" capital of Canada and, if it meant more money, perhaps even the world.

There is no official statement tacked on a wall of The Just One More Saloon listing all the things Manyberries doesn't have, although such a document is up for consideration. We haven't written a list as yet because we don't think any pilgrims passing through would spend two days reading it. I can tell you that one of the items on the unwritten list is a suburban golf course. We – that is, Big Tim Little and I – don't think we should have to wait until Manyberries gets its own suburbs before we acquire this essential attribute of prosperity and status.

Returning to the original subject of the discussion, Tim said that Newfoundland Premier Danny Williams was planning some sort of big celebration to mark the occasion of their newfound wealth. Ontario's Premier Dalton McGuinty was handing out crepe armbands to his citizens and wreaths were being hung on doors from Windsor to Ottawa.

"Danny Williams will blow so much money on a party to celebrate that next year they'll be back on hand-out corner," Perley said.

"We should have a big party to celebrate being the have-not capital of the world," Purvis said. "That might get Stephen and those guys in Ottawa paying attention and embarrass them into giving us our share."

"If we're not sending money down to Newfoundland anymore," Four-eyed Tom suggested, "maybe they could lower the taxes on beer and rye."

"I think we should just be grateful because Danny Williams says he has nothing more to say now that the election is over," I said. "Man, if he could sign a pact with Dalton McGuinty to that effect, the silence would be deafening."

Hazel was busy making sure that our various vessels were back in the "have" category. When she finished, she poked me on the shoulder, "Tell them what you said last night after everybody left about Danny Williams being like a bird."

"Well, I've reconsidered since then, and decided that, to be fair, most of the Premiers are like birds," I said to her. "What I told Hazel," I said, turning to my companions at the table, "was that Danny Williams should be called the Newfoundland Cardinal. But Stelmach and McGuinty share some of the same characteristics so I'd include them as well."

"Why a cardinal?" Tim asked. "Not that I've ever seen one."

"Well, the cardinal – the bird, not the religious type – will spend a lifetime pecking at mirrors to fend off an assumed enemy."

"It wouldn't cost a whole helluva lot if they lowered the taxes on beer and rye just for Manyberries," Tom said. "And the tax on gasoline and diesel."

"The government gives people living way up north allowances or tax breaks," Purvis said. "They should give a break to people living way down south." Purvis has long argued that if people living anywhere in Canada get isolation compensation, then so should everybody in Manyberries.

"I don't think your bird idea has legs, or wings, for that matter," Tim told me.

"What they could do is pay for free grocery deliveries from Medicine Hat," Perley offered. "Not the groceries, just the cost of trucking them down here. But we'd pay for our own gas when we go up there to play the VLTs and pick up groceries at the same time."

"It was several hours after you guys had gone home when I came up with the bird thing," I told Tim. "It was so late that it seemed inspirational at the time."

"You could try again in an hour, or maybe three, after everybody's had a lot more inspiration," he suggested. "If there's still a quorum."

The Manyberries Golf Tournament

The one important amenity we lack in Manyberries is a golf course. We don't have a lot of other things as well but some of us, well, certainly two of us, wish we had a golf course. For some reason, every time the Progressive Conservatives shovel out money to voters before an election, the shovel with the golf course money misses Manyberries.

On behalf of the golfing community I've raised this egregious government oversight several times at the Ranchmen's, even once when one of our politicians came to visit for a few minutes. There's still no sign of bulldozers on the horizon.

Up in Calgary they have golf courses scattered all over hell's half acre, which is pretty much what Calgary has become in recent years. They don't lack for golf courses in Calgary, or anything else for that matter, except a soul. I guess you could say that the golfers in Manyberries suffer from golf course envy.

That's not to say we won't golf. We are planning an annual tournament and even those who don't golf, which is everybody but Tim and me, will turn out for it.

Our facility is what you'd call a mobile golf course. It's a nine-holer with one tee-box and nine greens scattered out over the prairie beyond where the railroad tracks used to be.

Purvis and I had driven to Brooks with a few head of yearling calves he was selling and then went on to Calgary to look for bargains. Purvis loves to visit places where they sell fire-damaged goods and other insurance claim items at very low prices. He loads up the truck and brings them all back and sells whatever it is at a mark-up, for cash, that covers the cost of the fuel and other expenses. Sometimes you can get a couple of cases of canned beans or even fruit cocktail, all badly dented, that came from a semi-trailer that slid off the highway in a blizzard. Purvis buys them at 20 or 30 cents a can and sells them for double that.

On this trip, they were selling carpets that had suffered severe smoke damage in a warehouse fire. Purvis thought they'd be a big seller to people who smoke at home because when they wake up they can't even smell roses, let alone smoke damaged carpets, so he brought back a truckload.

I bought one to use as a putting surface in my backyard and that's what gave rise to the golf tournament. It was Perley who thought of it because he had been watching golf on satellite television in his intermittent quest to discover the point of the game.

He suggested we take all the carpets Purvis was unable to sell and scatter them out over the prairie at various distances from the platform where the train used to stop to let off passengers. Hardly anybody alive remembers when trains stopped and disgorged passengers but everybody knows it did happen from time to time in the last century. One of the old timers said he thought, but wouldn't swear to it, people stopped arriving by train around about the time they tore up the steel rails.

Perley said each carpet would represent a green and the golfers would tee off from the platform where we would nail down a carpet for the tee-box grass. We'd drive our balls from the platform at those prairie carpet greens and the winner would be the one whose balls were closest to the middle.

There were a couple of obstacles to overcome. One, I was the only person in town with golf clubs and I'm a left handed golfer. Tim has a set but he leaves them in Calgary. Two, I don't have very many golf balls since I left Ottawa and I hate buying them when I can find them. If each golfer hit nine balls out of the eleven I have, we'd spend a lot of tournament time running out and bringing them back.

Four-eyed Tom went home and dug around in his storage shed and came up with a solution. For reasons known only to Four-eyed, and perhaps not even him, he had more than 200 golf balls in a box along with a set of hickory-shafted golf clubs in a canvas bag.

Yet another obstacle presented itself and that was the colour of the balls: they were all the same colour. How would we identify whose ball was whose and who was closest to the flagstick on the greens?

Purvis came up with the solution by offering up all the cans of paint he's collected over the years and keeps stored in a shed out at his sons' ranch.

Each golfer would be responsible for selecting, painting his balls and then announcing his (or her if any of *them* wanted to participate) own personal colour. Four-eyed Tom chose robin egg blue and I took dark blue in memory of friends back in Ottawa. Perley chose pink while Purvis painted his balls black with a white stripe. When all the others had completed colouring their balls, we had a virtual rainbow.

We overcame the next obstacle by agreeing to use binoculars to watch each ball as it was hit to see where it landed. Three rotating judges with 12X binoculars would attest to the accuracy of each participant.

The next challenge was more difficult. Somebody asked how we'd get our balls back to the trainless station tee box and said there was no way he was going to walk out where there were rattlesnakes.

We hadn't thought of that because when we scattered the carpets we just threw them off the back of Purvis' truck and jammed sharpened diamond willow flag sticks through them. So there we were, with our balls scattered across the prairie and the likelihood of a first and only Cancelled Annual Manyberries Golf Tournament. If you don't have the balls for it, because of rattlesnakes, there's no way you'd be able to hold a second annual tournament because it too would have to be cancelled for lack of balls.

Four-eyed Tom came up with the solution: train the dogs to fetch our balls. It wouldn't be as easy as training them to fetch ducks or pheasants but with proper encouragement and huge chunks of top sirloin to reward them, we were sure it could be done.

Then Purvis raised another problem. It seems while he was training his dog, Three-eyed Tom, the biggest dog anybody ever saw, old Three-eyed developed an appetite for golf balls. Purvis would chip them across his backyard and tell Three-eyed Tom to fetch them. Three-eyed would stroll over to the ball, pick it up and swallow it. "He swallowed four of my balls," Purvis said, "before I quit training him. If he does that during the tournament, I'll run out of balls before the thing is barely underway."

Four-eyed Tom suggested that Purvis simply wait for nature to take its course and Three-eyed Tom would eventually return the balls. Purvis shook his head and said Four-eyed was welcome to come over to his backyard and be the first to hit the returned balls, when they were returned, to determine if they were still balanced.

Hazel said the Manyberries Golf Association should invest in a herd of Chihuahua dogs and train them to retrieve the balls because they couldn't possibly swallow a golf ball. Purvis countered that Three-eyed Tom could swallow Chihuahuas and probably would, thinking they were some sort of exotic rat, so that idea got shelved pretty quickly.

The last big challenge was of a wardrobe nature. Purvis and Perley said there was no way they'd golf without golf shoes like golfers on television wear. I have two pair of golf shoes, size 8. Purvis wears size 12 cowboy boots and Perley wears size 10 canvas high-top running shoes.

We're pretty confident that the inaugural tournament will be a go next year. Purvis is taking another truckload of calves to the packers in November and has volunteered to continue on up to Calgary. He'll visit his favourite insurance claim outlets and a few Salvation Army and Goodwill stores and buy four pairs of good condition golf shoes in various sizes. He'll rent them to the players for a modest fee to cover expenses.

I suggested he take Three-eyed Tom along and stroll around the many golf courses they have up in Calgary so Three-eyed could stock up on golf balls. He was amenable to that but said there was no way he was going to paint the balls when Three-eyed finally delivered them.

The Tourism Campaign

We had been reading a days-old copy of the Calgary Herald wherein it was reported that tourism in Calgary was flagging and the industry was worried. Hotel occupancy and summer reservations were down, both of which problems restaurant owners blamed on the cost of gasoline. We had to acknowledge that the world conspiracy to raise fuel prices here in Manyberries *was* being felt and that the cost of driving up to Medicine Hat to play the slot machines *was* beginning to hurt. We took some comfort in learning that even though Manyberries was no doubt the intended target of this nefarious plot, Calgary was suffering some spillover.

We decided something had to be done to boost tourism in Manyberries and pondered the dilemma long and hard over several cocktail hours.

I suggested that we bring in busloads of people who would like to get away from the asphalt jungle in places like Calgary. I told my colleagues that I had once been hunting around Rockyford, which is east of Calgary, or to be very precise, north of Manyberries, and discovered a novel tourist idea. I had stopped off in a very pleasant cocktail lounge in the town and was enjoying a jug at a table with several Hutterite gentlemen. I know a lot of Hutterites and while they don't hunt pheasants, they know where the birds hang out. They even sketched a map for me showing the best places. With their innate friendliness and hospitality, they're always willing to share such information with anyone who asks.

I was tucking the map in my shirt pocket when a wave of young people swept into the lounge. There were so many of them that three of the charming young women, and all the young women were charming, asked if they could sit at my table.

It turned out they were part of a group riding around in a bus that had left Calgary that morning on a one-day round trip. All the people aboard were from Saskatchewan and their tour was to take them to three country taverns before returning to Calgary. Rockyford was stop number two.

"We all live in Calgary now but most of us are from small towns in Saskatchewan and we do this two or three times a year as a way to get back to the country," one of the charming young women told me. She came from a farm where they have a huge pheasant population and said I should go there some hunting season.

"So," I told my cocktail hour friends, "there's the germ of an idea. We get busloads of people coming in to sample the wares of the Ranchmen's, with the added benefit of seeing acres and acres of nothing but emptiness and gophers between Calgary and here."

"Did she give you her name and tell you how to find her father's farm?" Perley asked. "Because if there are that many pheasants over there, maybe we could arrange a long weekend in Saskatchewan."

"She did, but I wrote it on a cigarette package that I tossed when it was empty. And I lost the map the Hutterites gave me when I put my shirt in the washing." Perley gave me a look of disgust that I could lose track of such important documents. "You're worse than Maxime Bernier."

"Not a bad idea," Purvis said, returning to my plan. "The cost of fuel on a per person basis wouldn't be all that much and if they're from Calgary, they have money to burn."

"That's a long drive, down here from Calgary," Tim said. "What are you going to do to entertain them between departure and arrival?"

"Well, the young woman said they stocked the bus with beer on ice so they had something to do between stops at all the taverns they visited. And I suppose they could listen to music. We're going after a younger demographic with this idea and young people don't read, don't vote and don't care. My guess is beer and music is all they want or need. And bags of chips and cheesies."

"I think we should do a test run," Purvis said, and Perley nodded agreement.

"We could borrow that old motor home from over on the east side," Perley said. "We could take it up to Seven Persons and invite people to travel down to Manyberries." Seven Persons is north of Manyberries, about halfway to Medicine Hat. The population is greater than seven.

"Who's gonna want to come down here from Seven Persons?" Four-eyed Tom asked. "They'll probably tell the driver to take them up to The Hat." Folks around here and even those who live there call their city The Hat.

"We'll get volunteers from here as our test tourists," Purvis said. "Anybody who wants to visit Manyberries will get on board some Saturday morning and enjoy the drive up to Seven Persons. All they'll have to bring is enough money for their share of the gasoline and whatever beer they'll need for the round trip."

"So what happens when we get back here from Seven Persons?" Perley asked.

"We'll make a grand entrance into the Ranchmen's and order beer," Purvis replied. "After we've had our fill, we'll pretend we're returning to Seven Persons but we'll really be returning the motor home. Then we'll come back here and discuss how successful the trip was and if it will work on a grander scale."

"Those tourism authorities in the other major urban centres can't hold a candle to what we've got going on here," Big Tim observed. "All they do is put cards in hotel rooms asking visitors what their impressions are of the city and what improvements they might suggest. This is a real hands-on study of what attracts tourists."

Purvis nodded modestly at Tim's praise. We could see that he was not just pleased but also proud of his contribution.

"What time would our test bus get back here?" Tom asked. "Would we be back by 11:00 am?"

"Not hardly," Purvis said. "We'd leave here at whatever time a Calgary tourist would find comfortable and convenient and get back about three hours after that. Probably up in Calgary they don't get out of bed much before noon on weekends."

"Then I can't go," Tom said. "I'm not going unless we can be here at 11:00 when Hazel opens the front door. That means we'll have to leave here no later than 7:30 which gives us a half hour to spare in case of breakdown." He got nods of agreement from everyone around the table, including Purvis.

"Tom," Big Tim said, "you've just exposed a major flaw here. You're the sort of individual, clear-headed, insightful and quick-witted, that the tourism industry could use."

He got nods of agreement around the table, including Tom.

"Maybe Hazel could advertise that happy hour starts when she opens and ends with the last person standing," I suggested.

"Two things wrong with that," Tim said. "First, Stelmach made happy hours illegal and second, if she could, and did, offer a two-for-one deal, there'd be no room in here for tourists."

Turning Turtle

"We're on the map," Purvis told me when I had settled into my chair. "We are reeeaallly on the world map."

"If I have to take notes, I hope you'll tell me how to spell 'really' when you stretch it out like that," I replied. "Anyway, what's the scoop?"

"Pregnant turtles," he said, "75-million-year-old pregnant turtles, and they came from Manyberries. Man, if this isn't finally the goose that lays golden eggs, I don't know what is." He was actually rubbing his hands like you see the villains do in 75-million-year-old movies on late night television.

He handed me two typed pages that came from Canoe on the internet. The headline read "Researchers discover fossilized pregnant turtle." In the body of the CP story the writer revealed the turtle was discovered near Manyberries by scientists and staff from the University of Calgary and the Royal Tyrrell Museum of Paleontology in Drumheller. Both those places are north of Manyberries.

"My grandson got that off his computer and as soon as I read it, I started seeing goldmines," Purvis informed me as I turned to wave at Big Tim Little and Perley, who'd just walked through the swinging doors. When they were settled I handed the news report to Tim.

"I read this on the internet this morning," he said, "and wondered if they'd dug up Old Rutherford's pet turtle that he must have buried when he was a young boy."

That drew a guffaw from Purvis. You can't find too many places on earth where they can out-guffaw Manyberrians. It's not that anybody dislikes Old Rutherford, it's just that he sort of dislikes everybody, so we enjoy a good snicker at his expense from time to time.

"We're gonna go digging for turtles, pregnant ones especially, and set up our own museum of pailingtoology," he announced, "and we're gonna sit back and watch the tourists and the money roll in."

"I dunno, Purvis, it'll be tough to compete with the Royal Tyrrell," Perley cautioned, "because they've got all those dinosaurs and other stuff."

Perley was exactly right. The Royal Tyrrell has dinosaurs and bones and stuff all over the place up there. It's world famous and sure put Drumheller on the map. It draws even more visitors than their penitentiary. If you want to visit Drumheller, just look at Manyberries on your map and then look north. It shouldn't be hard to locate.

"Yeah, but all they've got is this one turtle and its eggs. I bet there's a lot more where that one came from. We'll just find where they dug it up and when they're not there, we'll move in and dig up a whole herd of them."

"Where will you get the money for the museum? The governments are all in the red and cutting spending," Tim said. "And I doubt that Hazel will let you use one of her tables for a display."

"We'll use my little trailer, the one you guys call the eggshell. It does sort of look like an egg on wheels and it'd be perfect."

Purvis had bought the trailer from Old Rutherford and the Mrs, who are Manyberries' suntan parlour impresarios. They themselves had bought it from a young guy whose wife wouldn't stop having babies and therefore needed a much larger one for their vacations. O.R. and the Mrs had planned to tow it on a trip down through South America. He sold it to Purvis after Purvis told him about bandidos in Mexico preying on tourists. He made Purvis promise to sell it back when Mexico solves its crime problem. Purvis plans to tell him the bandidos were driven down into whatever country is south of Mexico when that happens.

"We'll set up a lawn chair with a picnic table and umbrella right at the door and charge them a dollar each to see our turtles," Purvis said. "And after I get my investment plus a little extra back from the trailer, it'll look like the pot of gold at the end of Finnegan's rainbow."

Big Tim looked at me and raised his eyebrows. I shook my head to indicate I didn't have an answer. Finnegan's rainbow? I decided to Google it if I remembered any of this in the morning.

"So what are the boys in the front room having?" Hazel asked when she finished her saunter from the bar to our table. "Same old same old, all around?" We all nodded yes.

"We're gonna set up a pregnant turtle museum," Purvis informed her. "Well, I am anyway. These guys will get free lifetime passes to it for helping me."

"Geez, I can't wait," she said. "Imagine, a pregnant turtle museum. They'll be flocking here all the way from Orion, maybe even Etzikom."

Orion is about 12 kilometres from Manyberries and the population is, officially: very few. Etzikom is a little further down the road.

"Don't laugh, Hazel," Purvis said, "these turtles are 75 million years old and so are their eggs."

"Will you put up a sign telling visitors that the turtles are 75 million years old and the eggs they laid are 75 million years old as well?"

"Sure, this is an educational sort of thing as well as a business venture," Purvis replied.

"Good. You'd want to be certain that people understood that if the turtle that laid the eggs did it 75 million years ago, that the eggs are at least that old as well." Hazel cleared our table of casualties and promised to return with additional recruits.

"I'll get my grandson to type up the signs on his computer," Purvis told her as she sauntered away. Nobody can saunter like Hazel.

"Says here that the turtle with eggs inside was found in 1999 and a nest with eggs in it was discovered 50 kilometres away six years later," Perley was reading the news story. "Will you be looking for nests with eggs, or turtles with eggs, or both, Purvis?"

"Both, the more we get the better. If we get enough nests, we can put some of my turtles on them so people can see what they looked like nesting. Maybe tack a few drawings of dinosaurs on the walls so people can see what the turtles were seeing when they were laying their eggs."

"You could maybe tack up a picture of Old Rutherford and the Mrs as well," Perley said, "to make it even more realistic."

"You can laugh now, Perley," Purvis said, "but when the tourists and dollars start rolling in, you'll be wishing you'd thought up this idea. It says here," and he pointed at the article, "that it was reported in some British journal called Biology Letters. Do you how many people live in England? Well, I don't either, but there's a lot. They'll be coming here from England by the busload to see it. Man, you can't get any better advertising than this."

"Don't forget China," Tim told him. "I read somewhere that they consider ancient eggs to be a real delicacy."

"How in hell are you gonna fry an egg that's turned into stone? If we just get the English, I'll make a fortune," Purvis replied.

Well, Manyberries still doesn't have a pregnant turtle and egg museum but not because Purvis has given up on it or lost his enthusiasm. It's just that every time he calls and asks us to go on an egg hunt, we always have to decline due to previous commitments.

And we have pledged never to reveal to Purvis that just over on the Montana side of the border, scientists more recently discovered a meat-eating dinosaur's nest with fragments of a dozen eggs. If we ever did, he'd be out shopping for a bigger trailer.

When the Vultures Come Home To Sing Castrato

It was five days after the death of the actor John Travolta's son that the Manyberries camel finally buckled. Nobody, among those of us who gather daily at The Just One More Saloon, had even mentioned it but I'm certain that each of us paused to reflect quietly on a profound sorrow we knew was shrouding the Travolta household.

Big Tim raised it first when he said he was about ready to throw a brick at his television set the previous night when yet another of the endless, breathless, hour-by-hour reports about the death popped up on one of those entertainment programs that pass themselves off as newscasts.

I had to ask him which one because even what passes for regular news programs on Canadian television were including the Travolta story in their lineups, and fairly high up on those lineups at that. I'd read of the death on the internet and after that did my best to ignore it, knowing that by the time the media finished with it, which would take a month at least, those old familiar feelings of creeping nausea would be hitting me. I love my channel switcher because now that Canadian television news programs are doing their best to look and sound American, they tell you what's coming right after the commercial break. If I'm not interested, I hit the button which takes me to the History Channel where I can watch reruns of World War Two.

Tim said that all the media, including those simpering insipid shouters on the entertainment programs, made him want to puke. He had been talking to Hazel when I arrived about the wall-to-wall coverage and wondering why the media wouldn't leave the Travolta family alone. Hazel said they were treating it as news because the vast majority of Canadians and Americans are stupid, dull and believe whatever they're told, and if the media says it's news, then the chronically dull and stupid believe them.

When they asked me what I thought, I said vultures, Turkey Vultures to be precise, or *Cathartes aura*, if you want their scientific name. Not very many people will ever see a Turkey Vulture in the wild, at least not up close. But here in Manyberries we often see them in the summer months, soaring far overhead on the thermals, watching for the carcasses on which they feed. What little I've read about them says their heads are featherless so that when they feed, nothing sticks to them. I told my friends the only difference between the bird and the so-called journalists who cover tragedies like the Travolta death are the bald heads. The human vultures are all perfectly coiffed. But their feeding habits are remarkably similar, as well as their absolute ignorance or disregard for what the more discerning might consider tasteful or appetizing.

"What got me last night," Tim said, "was some guy yelling at me on one of the programs that he'd be right back to tell me what I was feeling about the boy's death. And they do yell! That's when I hit the off button and hoped somebody castrates the twerp soon before he can breed any more of whatever it is they are."

"I think, considering the pitch of their voices, most of them on those shows have already had that done," Hazel said. "And the women are just as shrieky as the men."

"Twerpy Vultures," I said, "not bad Tim, not bad at all."

"Why do they have to cover this stuff like it's World War Three?" Hazel asked. "Sure, John Travolta is an actor, famous and all that, but he's a father and he lost a son and these people treat him like he's only a *thing*, or a piece of a thing, and not a real person. Don't they have any heart at all?"

"I like it," I started to say but then corrected myself, "no, I don't like it, because I cringe in embarrassment and disgust when they do it, but it's when some reporter armed with a microphone and backed by a camera and no brains asks somebody who's just lost a loved one how he or she feels. It gets worse if the grieving person tries to answer. But it gets better for the cameras if the griever breaks down and cries because then they'll zoom in for a close-up that they'll run for as many days as they can."

"And people will stop what they're doing to watch that on television," Hazel said, "which proves my argument that we've got runaway growth in the stupid population."

Toronto the Good, Bad & Ugly

"Living in Toronto must be an awful drag on the spirit," Big Tim Little said as I painfully eased myself into my chair. I had just returned from a three day tour around southern Alberta with the Manyberries Unprofessional Golf Association and had a need for a full body splint. The rest of my foursome, non-golfers, went along as travelling companions and happily spent their time and money in the lounges of the courses we visited while I unhappily flailed away under a blistering hot prairie sun. Purvis, Perley and Four-eyed Tom think that golf is a waste of time when the courses have lounges with actual cocktail menus. For some of us, this is on the list of the most important things you should do before you die. I've seen people in Toronto lounges agonize over cocktail menus for as long as they do the food menus, visibly aging as they do. Here at The Just One More we have no need for such superfluities because we all know what we drink.

"Just *talking* about Toronto is an awful drag on the spirit," I said. "Even looking at maps that show the location of Toronto sometimes throws me into a blue funk."

"It's probably the most repressive city in the world," Tim said. "They've got bylaws to cover every eventuality and probably bylaws to cover eventual eventualities. Do you want me to wave at Hazel for you? You look like you could use a litre of oil to get that wreck of a thing you call a body functioning again."

"Wine'll be fine," I said. "What's this about Toronto?"

Tim hauled out two full pages from a recent National Post with a blaring headline: "Is Toronto The Nanny State Capital Of Canada?" There were colour photos of junk food, balloons, a young woman talking on a cell phone, a car's exhaust pipe and a park bench. "It says here they're even contemplating regulating how much shade has to be provided in all their city parks," and he pointed at a paragraph on the inside page which was headlined "Nanny State Beckons". Tim emptied his glass with a long gulp and looked around for Hazel to bring replacements. "Geez, living there must be like living under a heavy wet wool blanket."

One paragraph that caught my eye said Toronto City Hall had created a bureaucracy of inspectors to make sure Torontonians who filed for rebates on dual flush toilets weren't cheating. People who bought dual flush got a $75 rebate while cheapskates who bought lower-efficiency models only got $60 back. I did a quick calculation and figured Toronto probably spent $20 per hour for each inspector to visit homes all over the city to make sure nobody made a sneaky $15 profit. I've driven in Toronto and can testify that it takes more than an hour to drive anywhere.

"Well, you know back a long time ago, the socialists had an idea that if they couldn't win elections at the provincial and federal levels, they could start at the municipal level and work their way up." I thanked Hazel for delivering my lubricant and asked if she had any WD-40 behind the bar. She told me if I wanted to hang around until closing time she'd be happy to hose me down with the stuff. I told her that in my condition even removing my shirt was too painful and asked her for a rain cheque. She told me snoozers are losers and went back to the bar.

"They quote some expert in this story who says the danger is that people will wind up thinking the government is there to do everything for them and that they don't have to assume any responsibility at all for their actions or decisions," Tim said. "They even put warning signs up in playgrounds telling parents they have to supervise their kids' play. Can you imagine a whole gang of yappy Toronto mommies and daddies badgering their kids about how to slide or swing safely? Kids'll grow up whiny, timid and probably voting NDP."

"Maybe it's in the Ontario water," I said. "In Ottawa they won't let people put their garbage out in those small plastic grocery bags because it means more bending for the garbage collectors. That means you've either gotta save all your garbage until you can fill a big green bag or stuff it in the neighbour's green bag when nobody's watching."

Tim nodded and waved at Perley, Purvis and Four-eyed Tom, who were arriving late for the cocktail hour. Visiting all those golf courses on our recent tour had taken a toll and their afternoon naps had to be extended because of it.

"We're discussing the sorry state of Toronto," Tim informed them, "and how the city is turning into a cradle to grave nanny state. They're even planning to regulate how much shade there has to be in every city park."

"We should have a park in Manyberries," Four-eyed said. "I could sit there some afternoons instead of on my flatbed out on the street."

"If we got a park," Purvis said, "the next thing you know somebody would be demanding that it have trees and benches. That's an expensive slippery slope you're on, Tom."

"And then somebody would want a law forcing people to clean up after their dogs in the park," Perley said, "and who could tell one dog's leavings from another?"

"Says here that in Montreal shopkeepers are forbidden to sweep the sidewalks in front of their establishments even though the law says they must," I said. "Seems the city workers went to arbitration and argued that sweeping sidewalks is their responsibility, even if they never do it."

"Yeah, but Montreal is sort of like an old aunt who's a little off her rocker but harmless," Big Tim said. "Toronto is more like an old aunt who gets the vapours whenever there's a bit of excitement."

"I could never live in Toronto," Four-eyed Tom told us.

"That's true Tom, you never could," I replied. "They have bylaws down there."

"But we shouldn't be too smug," Tim said, "after all we've got a law regulating happy hours in bars. Where else would they pass a law saying there are certain hours where nobody's allowed to be happy?"

Forever in Cow Genes

"Do you remember when I had the idea of inventing some sort of contraption to bag and save cow gas?" Purvis asked as I leaned back for a surprisingly on-time inventory delivery from Hazel.

"Was that the time you figured we could be as big or bigger than Shell and Petro-Canada if we sold the cow gas for home heating and cigarette lighter fuel?"

"Yeah, that was it, but forget about that, I've got something bigger." Purvis waited while Big Tim, Perley and Four-eyed Tom bellied up to the table and squirmed and shifted to find their grooves.

"My grandson gave me this thing off his computer," he said, and waved two sheets of paper at us. "It says cows may hold the secret for unleashing energy in corn."

"The cows in those feedlots are already releasing a lot of energy when they're being fattened and finished on corn," Big Tim said. "I waste a lot of energy trying to stay upwind of those places."

"This scientific guy," Purvis went on, ignoring Big Tim, "took a gene from a cow and put it in a corn cell. He says that'll make the stalks, leaves and probably even the bare cobs I'd guess more valuable. All that stuff can be used to make cheap ethanol."

"Ethanol?" Four-eyed Tom asked. "Is that the same as the stuff I get from my still? It'd be a lot cheaper and easier to boil up the stalks instead of scraping all those kernels off the cobs."

"No, it'd probably be even more dangerous to drink that stuff than yours, Tom," Perley said. "But you could probably use it instead of gas in your old flatbed."

Big Tim had scanned Purvis' scientific business plan and handed it to me. "Looks like a sound proposition to me, Purvis," he said. "All we have to do is get one of those genes from a cow and stick it in some corn and we're away to the races." Tim has two degrees that he actually went to university to get so we defer to him on matters such as these. He's retired but still does a lot of consulting with big oil companies about underground stuff which he knows about because of those degrees.

"That's what I was thinking," Purvis said. "We get some sort of scraping machine to clean the cobs, sell the kernels to a feedlot and use the rest to make ethanol."

"But Purvis," Perley interrupted, "we couldn't grow enough corn in these parts to feed people, let alone enough to feed cows."

"You're a small thinker, Perley," Purvis said. "You're right of course, but who needs to grow it when we can let those guys up around Taber do it for us?"

"Where do we get the genes from," Tom wondered. "I mean how many genes would a cow hold?" He turned to Tim, our academic advisor and scientific guru.

"I'd think, but can't say for certain, that one cow would hold a lot of genes," Tim said. "Maybe millions of genes, but you couldn't extract them all or there'd be no cow."

"My sons are running 750 head of cows," Purvis said. "If we took only a few thousand genes per cow, we'd have enough to do most of the corn in Alberta."

"How are you gonna get the cow genes into the corn stalks?" Perley asked.

"I figure we hire school kids to do it. We give them all hypodermic needles and set them loose in the corn fields. They squirt a bit of this gene stuff into every stalk and refill the needle from a jar they'll be carrying."

"Then, after harvest, you pay the farmer for the stalks left standing?"

"No, hell, we'll offer to clear their fields of all that fodder for free, ship the stuff to a refinery and distill it and sell it."

"My still gives me two quarts in 12 hours," Tom said, "and it takes nearly two quarts of gas to drive here and back every day. Sounds like you'll need a pretty big still, Purvis."

"Well, these are details. It's like a jigsaw puzzle where you know from the big picture what it's supposed to look like and all you have to do is sort through the pieces, the details, and put them together."

"This is what made Canada what it is today, Purvis," Tim said. "It's dreamers like you with restless, searching souls who have put our country out standing in a field."

All Roads Lead to Manyberries

"Exactly what I was thinking," Purvis said. "And you guys heard it first."

"I'm not going to waste the stuff from my still driving back and forth between home and here everyday," Four-eyed Tom told us.

Safing the World

"Did you hear about that young guy down in Vermont who bought a Whopper?" Perley was grinning and twitching with excitement over his news.

"Perley, if I had to hear about every young guy who bought a Whopper, I'd have to devote my life to listening," I replied and waved at Hazel to let her know she could begin curb side service whenever the fancy struck her.

"No, no, this is one young guy and did he ever get a surprise when he bit into it."

"I don't want to hear the story right now if what he found involves anything to do with body parts, even cow body parts," I said. "In fact I don't want to hear the story ever because the older I get the queasier I get."

"It was a condom," Perley said, "an unwrapped condom," and handed me a copy of a story by the Associated Press that somebody had printed from *cnews* from Canoe.ca. Purvis took it before I finished scanning it.

"When did you get a computer?" I asked.

"I didn't. My son sent me that. He has one of the damned things and gets stuff off it like this. I might get one myself if they run good stories like this."

"What brand of condom?" Four-eyed Tom asked.

"What the hell does it matter what the brand was," Purvis said. "A condom is a condom, unless you find it in your hamburger and then it's a ticket to a windfall. And it says here the guy is suing whoever it is who makes Whoppers, whatever they are."

"I was just reading the other day that a good journalist asks who, what, why, when and where, so what *brand* of condom must be important," Tom protested.

"You thinking about a post-retirement career in journalism, Tom?" I asked. "Because if you are, you better be prepared to enter a world of murk, mystery and mob mentality."

"The guy discovered it on his third bite," Perley explained. "Said he detected a 'foreign taste, a very sour, bitter sort of taste that almost had a numbing sensation,' so he bit down even harder."

"Wait a minute, hold on," I said. "The guy tasted something sour, bitter and numbing and he still went on eating?"

"Well, he's a young guy and they have big appetites and he was probably pretty hungry. Anyway, when he bit down even harder he felt something rubber-like grind between his teeth and that's when he pulled his hamburger back from his mouth."

"And that's when he saw the condom, hanging out of the burger?" Big Tim asked. "I'd guess that'd put just about anybody off the rest of his meal."

"No, it was hanging out of his mouth because it was stuck between his teeth."

As I recall, it was just about then I thought I'd have to start banging my forehead on the table to stop laughing. Purvis handed me the paper.

"If I was his girlfriend, that'd sure put me off giving him a smooch," Big Tim said. "Probably for a long, long time. Maybe forever, if she couldn't stop laughing."

"Anyway, he's suing somebody," Perley went on. "For pain, suffering, emotional distress and medical expenses. His lawyer says he passed a lie detector test with flying colours."

"If they go to court, they'll have to take the condom as evidence," Four-eyed observed, "so then we can find out what brand it was."

"Now you're talking," Purvis said. "Can you imagine how a young fella would feel if he was sitting in a hamburger joint with a condom hanging out of his mouth and everybody looking at him? It's gotta be worth millions."

"Well, actually, it says he bought it to take home to eat and he was all alone at the time."

"That should teach us something," Purvis said, "Always eat your hamburger where you bought it. If there's nobody around to see how embarrassed you are to have a condom hanging out of your mouth you can't sue for nearly as much."

"If it was unwrapped, I don't suppose they'll ever know what brand it was," Four-eyed said.

"It says here he has what's left of the hamburger, its original wrapper and the condom in a baggy in his freezer," I said. "Since he has the evidence, all your questions will be answered when it goes to court."

"So what are the boys in the front room warring over tonight?" Hazel asked and began placing our individual allotments of ammunition in front of us.

"Some young guy in the States chewed a condom that came out of a hamburger he bought," Purvis told her, "and we're wondering how much he'll get if he sues somebody."

"I think being in the middle of cattle country," Hazel said, "you should be wondering and worrying more whether the Americans are experimenting with meat substitutes or going vegetarian."

Dinosaurs and Aliens

"I've got another reason why we should go ahead with my turtles and eggs museum," Purvis informed us as we gathered for the March cocktail hour. "We can add kitten-sized dinosaurs."

Purvis had been reading a Calgary Herald story about the discovery of an eensy-teensy dinosaur by Alberta paleontologists. They found it in a box at the University of Alberta. This is not to say that it crawled in there and expired, because the U of A isn't that ancient. The fossil had been sitting encased in rock in the box after being placed there several decades earlier. It had been found at Dinosaur Provincial Park in 1982 and only recently unboxed and analyzed.

The experts said it would have been smaller than a housecat, weighing in at two kilograms and standing about 50 centimetres tall. It also packed razor-sharp claws and "teeth like daggers," according to the researchers.

I had already read the story on line and seen the rendition of what it looked like and done my own research. TLC (The Last Cat) is not 50 centimetres tall. I don't know how much he weighs because he wouldn't stay on the bathroom scale long enough to check his weight, but he's a helluva lot more than two kilograms. Being as scientific as possible I picked him up and then picked up a 2.12 kg package of ground turkey and could feel there was no comparison.

"So, if you could get one, would you say that these were the stone-age equivalent of cats that people kept in their caves to chase mice?" I asked. "Something for stone-age kids to play with and tease?"

"I never thought of that, but it's a good idea anyway," Purvis said and took out his shirt pocket spiral bound notebook and wrote down kids and kittens. "But I was thinking about how we might throw in another attraction for people who aren't interested in old turtles and eggs."

"Well, apart from an estimated several thousand people I've met over the years, that still leaves a lot of people who like cats and kittens, so you might be on to something here," I said, steepling my hands and bowing my head in thanks to Hazel for giving us that which we were grateful to receive. Everyday is Thanksgiving Day at The Just One More Saloon.

"But I've got another idea that might drag in a third bunch," Purvis said. "Aliens. Everybody's interested in aliens like, you know, that E.T. thing in the movies some time back."

His idea came to him, Purvis said, when he read a headline about aliens coming to Canada as bogus refugees and that got him thinking about a conversation he had had with Four-eyed Tom.

"I went duck hunting with Tom last October," he explained. "And after we got the decoys out and settled in to wait for daylight, Tom started talking about things flying around up in space. He can be spooky when he starts in on things like that and said he thought there were space ships up there that could come down and snatch a guy right out of his duck blind and nobody would ever know." Purvis paused to check the bouquet of his Pilsner and take a small sip to see if it was acceptable. He nodded his approval to Hazel who ran her middle finger down from her forehead to the tip of her nose and left it there to indicate her relief and pleasure that it met his standards.

"Anyway, then he got started on how he always wondered if there might be things, aliens and such, at the bottom of sloughs. He said he'd seen enough movies on television about creatures coming up out of swamps to convince him they could also be hiding in sloughs."

"Remind me," I said, "next autumn to not go duck hunting with Tom. Or any place when it's dark."

"See, what I figured was I'd get somebody like Thor to sit down with Tom and draw what he imagines one of these space aliens or slough swamp critters would look like." Thor has another name but we call her that because she resembles the lady in operas who wears a helmet with horns and carries a trident; the one who sings at the very end. Thor also has pigtails which she has worn since her teenage years and has never been seen wearing anything on her feet but heavy work boots. She graduated some years ago from a calligraphy correspondence course and does a lot of work for people in the area, designing yard and garage sale signs. Thor was born, raised and married in Manyberries. Oldtimers remember when she was just a slip of a girl but Thor slipped past that description a long time ago.

"Then, once we have drawings from his imagination, we get the kids over at the school to build the things out of old newspapers and flour paste."

"As fearless as she is, I'm not sure even Thor could muster the inner fortitude to keep from running and screaming in horror if she heard Four-eyed Tom reveal whatever it is he keeps closeted, thank God, in his mind."

"Yeah, but anything that's half as scary as what he thinks would probably draw huge crowds. It's like me, I'm afraid of snakes but I can't *not* look at pictures of them, like rattlesnakes, and especially those ones in India that can spit in your eye at 30 feet." Purvis shuddered at the mere thought of snakes and I did the same in sympathy.

"Maybe you could put Tom on display in your museum and he could tell visitors some of the things he imagines," Hazel suggested. "But on second thought," and she gestured at me, "he could be right that whatever Tom might imagine and describe at any given time could be too horrible to contemplate, let alone hear, for sane people."

We're Short Skilled People

Old Rutherford came in clutching his ancient briefcase and looking glum. He always looks glum but this evening he looked glummer than usual. It is not often Old Rutherford deigns to socialize with us colonials during the famous and much envied Manyberries cocktail hour, but when he wants something he does. And for several months now Old Rutherford has wanted something.

Manyberries is facing a crisis similar to other major centres in Canada: we have an extreme skilled labour shortage. On top of that we don't even know precisely how critical our skilled labour shortage is. We do know two things: that if Manyberries had its own telephone book, it would be a quarter page followed by no yellow pages where you could look up and contact a tradesman.

Yes, most of us know how to hotwire a pickup when we lose the keys and everybody in town knows how to screw in a light bulb. But when it comes to somebody who actually went to a school somewhere to learn about electricity we have nada. Nobody. At least nobody anybody knows about.

Same thing with plumbers. Most of us are handy with plungers and know how to pour Liquid Plumber down the drain but we're not certain there's anybody in town who actually studied the science and physics of plumbing.

Old Rutherford had been studying this problem for quite some time after reading something in a Calgary Sun he got gratis from the men's room. Up in Calgary the government was reported to have funded a study to determine the cause and recommend solutions to their labour shortage. Old Rutherford almost swallowed his tongue when he read that hamburger flippers are making over 12 bucks an hour. He nearly swallowed his pride as well by thinking about retiring from retirement and moving to Calgary to get a job in the fast food industry.

It was after reading the Sun that he came to our table one evening with a proposition that he said would finally fulfill Manyberries' destiny. We were so busy fulfilling our own destinies, with help from Hazel at the bar, that we almost ignored him. Until he mentioned government grants.

"It seems to me," he said at that time, "that Manyberries should have an accurate picture of just what the obstacles are that stand in the way of expanding our industrial base."

"Our industrial base is where we are right now," Big Tim Little said. "We're in the industrial heart of Manyberries. It's called the Southern Ranchmen's Inn." If Tim had been a little more precise he would have added that the sign outside also says this is The Just One More Saloon.

"I'm well aware of that," Old Rutherford said, "and the trailer the Mrs and I have with that sun tanning equipment is the other. But I'm talking about industry where they actually have land set aside for warehouses, factories, shipping and trucking facilities and etc. with skilled people inside them doing skilled work."

"Don't all those big trucks rolling through with loads of pipe or cows count, when the drivers stop for a beer?" Four-eyed Tom asked. "Sometimes when those guys are deadheading it, they even spend the night in their tractor bunks. Some nights it looks like a shipping and trucking centre out front." We ignored Tom because we knew Old Rutherford was talking about permanent structures.

"I'm suggesting we apply to Mr. Ed Stelmach for a grant to research our skilled labour market to determine where the shortages are most critical and what the government can do to address those shortages. The study would be funded by the government and the actual survey done by the Manyberries Chamber of Commerce."

"We don't have a Chamber of Commerce," Perley said. "We don't have a chamber of anything. Unless you count that antique chamber pot in our kitchen where my wife grows herbs. There is no commerce around here."

"That doesn't mean we can't get a grant from the government," Purvis said. Purvis has this obsession about governments that requires some explanation. It grieves him that the federal government claws back all his Old Age Security payments. He finally consulted with an accountant who is a master chef with the books of a major oil company and even he wasn't able to juggle his figures so that Purvis could get at least a portion back of the OAS. His quest is to find a way to get something, anything, from any government to compensate.

So at Old Rutherford's urging we became the Manyberries Chamber of Commerce. Purvis agreed to sign on as Chairman; Perley assumed responsibility as Vice-President, Industrial Sector Issues; Four-eyed Tom agreed to chair the Retail Sector Committee; Big Tim Little became Chair of the Entrepreneurial Development Committee, because he was the only one around who could spell entrepreneurial; and I took on duties as Media Outreach Director. Old Rutherford would be the Recording Secretary and Government Relations Coordinator. That meant that any real work, like writing a letter to government, would be done by him.

I must say the letterhead Old Rutherford designed on his ancient upright Underwood looked pretty official. He had very carefully clipped letters out of newspapers to spell out Manyberries Chamber of Commerce across the top and ran all our names and titles down the left hand side. After he persuaded the secretary over at the school to photocopy the original draft it looked almost as good as anything you'd find up in Calgary.

To make the survey of the Manyberries labour shortage legitimate, Old Rutherford talked to residents from one end of town to the other, close to 100 of them. He usually doesn't talk to colonials, what with having been born in England and all.

Purvis says Old Rutherford is like every other Brit, even the Cockneys; they're superior beings when they arrive here. Purvis says every Brit who comes here immediately runs for something so they can all end up running everything.

"Take Bob Rae, for instance," he said. "The guy arrives here from England and immediately starts running for the NDP and winds up running Ontario."

"But Purvis," I said, "Bob Rae didn't arrive, he returned to Canada after attending Oxford. He was actually born Canadian."

"Yeah, well, so they got him over there and propaganded him into becoming an Englishman," Purvis replied. "Same difference."

But Old Rutherford shed his prejudices and talked to everybody. If it takes 98 percent of the population to give you a credible cross-sample of opinions, he delivered. He didn't interview himself and the Mrs to avoid any suspicion of bias.

He pulled it all together, wrote an executive summary and drew up graphs and pie charts so diligently that you would have been proud to take that proposal to Edmonton, maybe even to Ottawa. The summary, in essence, said Manyberries has a huge skilled labour shortage that would likely continue into the foreseeable future unless we attracted some critically important industry. The request was for $100,000 to cover the cost of the survey to date and a further half million to create and execute a program to attract the industries that would in turn draw skilled labour to Manyberries like sour milk draws flies. The half million would cover per diems and expenses for the volunteer Manyberries Chamber of Commerce search committee.

"Mr. Ed Stelmach wrote me a letter," Old Rutherford told us and opened his battered old briefcase. He had purchased it at a flea market in Medicine Hat after he retired. He'd never had need for one during his career as a shipper and receiver for an agricultural implements business but believes that a briefcase gives a man a certain panache.

"It says they can't possibly fund our project because of their election pledge to manage our taxes as if the dollars were their very own."

Purvis snorted and shook his head. "It's revenge is what it is," he said. "They're getting even with us because somebody here voted Liberal," and he looked at me, "and two more voted New Democrat and for the Green Party," and he pointed at Perley and then himself. "See how a good joke can backfire?"

"Our tax dollars *are* their own," Big Tim said. "There wasn't anything left after those guys in the government blew open the vault for those raises they gave themselves."

"It's a damn shame," Perley said, "that we've elected a government so short-sighted it can't see the value of an industrial complex this close to the American border."

"It's too bad," Four-eyed Tom said, "because I was hoping we could get a barber here so I wouldn't have to drive all the way up to Medicine Hat every year."

Carbonated Cows

We were a little surprised to find Purvis already settled in his chair when we arrived for the Official Manyberries Cocktail Hour. It was the day they swore in Stephen Harper's new Cabinet. We assumed, wrongly, that Purvis had decided to discuss who got what portfolio and who didn't get anything.

Usually, Purvis likes to arrive a few minutes after the rest of us so he can make an entrance. Purvis wouldn't call it that because he wouldn't know what it means but he does like to come in looking rushed and muttering about stockbrokers, investments and how so much of his time is spent handing out free advice to world experts. We worry that one day he might spot some of those self-important types you see in the cities wearing those cellular phone things permanently attached to their ears. In Ottawa that's a dead giveaway that you want people to think they're looking at somebody who's on the Prime Minister's speed dial. In Toronto it signals that the barons of Bay Street won't sleep well if they can't reach you when nickels need squeezing. In Calgary it tells the world that you don't have time to join the Petroleum Club but might entertain an invitation if somebody from there ever calls. In Vancouver it means you're a waiter or waitress hoping your agent calls about a bit part in a cheap made-in-Canada American movie.

We had only just pulled up our chairs and given Hazel a big smile when Purvis asked if we knew how much time we wasted by gathering every day except Sunday to think about things.

"I've never given it any thought," I said, "but if pressed, I'd guess the answer would be 100 percent."

"I didn't bring my slide rule," Tim offered, "so I can't do a precise calculation but I'd say something like 111 percent of the time I've spent here so far has been wasted."

"Like Ian Tyson once sang, 'If I could roll back the years,' I'd guess most of the best of them were wasted here," Perley said and thanked Hazel for her assistance. "Of course, one man's waste is another man's compost."

"I work on my crossword puzzles," Four-eyed Tom told us, "and I've got a shedful of finished ones to show for the hours I spend here."

Strictly speaking what Tom said was true, but thousands of hours spent learning and/or memorizing words by doing crossword puzzles hasn't done much for him in the sparkling conversationalist category.

"Do you guys know how many hours we've wasted talking about cow farts and how to make money off them?" Purvis asked. "Well, I don't either, but it's plenty. And all this time we wasted talking about cow *farts* when we should have been talking about cow *burps*. That's where the money is."

Purvis hauled out a computer printout of a news story and handed it to me. The headline was "Less grass, less gas, says cattle researcher" and it was written by a Linda Shepertycki of Canwest News Service. It was datelined Winnipeg but had been carried in the Ottawa Citizen.

"My grandson found that on the computer," Purvis commented. "It says in there that some scientific guy has discovered that cows burp a lot more than they fart if they're fed grass. In fact, he says 98 percent of the methane that comes out of a cow is through its mouth and only two percent comes from the other end!"

"Eructation of the bovine nation," Tim said and handed the story to Four-eyed Tom who passed it on to Perley without looking up from his crossword.

"I've been to Winnipeg many times and always wondered what it is they actually do there," I said.

"But here's the thing," Purvis said, "we're always talking about inventing a contraption to capture cow farts so we can sell the gas as heating or cigarette lighter fuel. We've been looking at this thing from the wrong end, and this guy's already got a contraption for getting it straight from the cow's mouth. They're miles ahead of us over there."

"It'll embarrass the hell out of Ed Stelmach and his Government when they read about this," Tim said. "We're supposed to be the energy experts in Canada."

The story said this scientific guy, Ermias Kebreab by name, and I did not make that up, has been studying dairy cow emissions for four years. He works at the National Centre for Livestock and the Environment, an establishment nobody around the table had ever heard of.

The reporter witnessed first hand a demonstration whereby an old Jersey steer named George stuck his head into a Plexiglass feeding compartment. He had a hooded collar around his neck to trap whatever gas he emitted inside the compartment. A hose captured the gas and transferred it to a measuring machine. Turns out old George, when he eats grass, produces 600 to 700 litres of methane per day, but only 500 when he's on an all-grain diet.

"Can you imagine the time we would have wasted if we had backed our cows into compartments instead of herding them in head-first?" Purvis asked. "Or if we had invented a rear-end contraption instead of a front-end one? Look at my calculations there on the bottom of the page."

I looked at his scrawl and saw that Purvis had 650 multiplied by two and then divided by 100 to equal 13.

"This scientific guy's figures indicate we'd get only 13 litres out of one cow if we had gone through with our plan when we could have been getting 600 to 700 from the opposite end."

"Helluva way to blow your profit potential," Tim agreed.

"But here's the thing. The other day my grandsons were drinking Coke and having a burping contest. Geez, those guys could pass for volcanoes. If we switched the cows to Coca-Cola instead of water and fed them grass only, we could probably double their output."

"And there'd probably be a specialty market after we slaughter them," Perley suggested. "A lot those city folks would probably jump at the chance to eat carbonated cow meat."

"But what if it made them burp?" Four-eyed Tom wondered.

"Gas masks," Purvis said. "We could take old surplus gas masks and convert them into burp traps for the city folks to wear. Man, there's no end to the possibilities."

Terrorist Cow Flaps

Purvis asked me when I walked in on Monday if I had run for cover when the terrorists attacked up in Calgary. When somebody, especially Purvis, asks you a question like that you tend to hesitate before answering, and you should probably resist asking what he means. If he's making a joke it could be one he memorized, rehearsed and practised in front of a mirror for hours to get it just right. Some of the jokes are rather lengthy and, depending on how long he's been sitting in The Just One More, he often forgets the punch line, an affliction not unfamiliar to the rest of us. It gets worse when we remember only the punch line because then it takes a lot of concentration to create a story line to precede it.

But this time it was about the wave of panic that had hit Calgary on a weekend when I was visiting. It was one of those pleasant autumn days with a light Chinook breeze coming in from the west, the sort of day when anybody with even a hint of common sense would be out hunting pheasants.

It was, after a few chilling weeks and the early onslaught of snow, warm enough that a host could invite his guest to sit out on the back deck without fear of the merlot freezing in the glass. We had just got seated when I got a whiff of an old familiar scent coming from beyond the western city limits: either a farmer running his manure spreader or a feedlot operator scraping out the corrals. We continued our conversation, pausing occasionally to savour what was once called the smell of money in Alberta.

That was the background to the question Purvis asked about terrorists. He had heard a report on a Calgary radio station that people were calling the city hotline, 311, anxiously wondering what was making that very strange, and perhaps dangerous, smell. Purvis said if they were calling 311 they must have been in such a panic that they were probably calling 911 or even the Emergency Preparedness Office and maybe the military as well.

"Geez, they don't know what manure smells like," Purvis exclaimed in disgust. "And those guys call themselves cowtowners!"

"Probably most of them came in from Toronto or some other place and have't left the city since they arrived unless it was on a plane," Perley suggested. "If they never smelled it at home and never go anywhere but to Banff, how would they know what the smell is?"

"Yeah, but then the media got on to it and even the workers who answer the help line didn't know what it was. Now, you'd think that anybody working for the City of Calgary should at least have to know what manure smells like."

"Especially considering what they've got for a City Council up there," Big Tim Little said. "Working that close to that bunch you'd think they recognize it right off the bat."

"Well, I knew what it was at the first sniff," I said.

"Not surprising considering where you worked in Ottawa," Perley told me. "They keep the spreaders on standby down there."

"Guess I must have left for home before the news hit the fan," I said. "And I was listening to Willy Nelson and Ian Tyson on CDs so didn't hear any reports about the citizens going into a flap over the smell of cows. But I did pick up a story that I thought warrants closer scrutiny. It's about piddling passengers on airplanes."

"I'd rather listen to Willy and Ian," Four-eyed Tom said and went back to his crossword puzzle book.

"This little story," I explained, laying the printout on the table, "says All Nippon Airways in Japan is asking passengers to relieve themselves before boarding to reduce the weight the plane will be carrying."

"You mean number one and two?" Purvis asked.

"Just number one, according to this report. They calculate that if every passenger drains before boarding they'll knock 63.7 kilograms off the load for each flight."

"Says here," Tim was reading the story, "that attendants will stand by the boarding gate and ask the passengers if they'll be kind enough to relieve themselves before boarding."

"What, they're gonna stand there with a bucket and make everybody pee before they board?" Purvis shook his head. "Sounds like something Air Canada would do, or would have done back when the government owned the outfit."

"If some stewardess was standing there with a bucket and there were people lined up behind me, I don't think I could do it." Four-eyed told us. You never know, when he's working on his crosswords, if Tom is paying attention.

"All you'd have to do is stop off at the lounge and have a few beers, Tom, before you get to the boarding gate and you won't have a problem," Tim assured him.

I should mention that Tom has never been to a foreign country, except Montana, because he refuses to board an airplane. He has always wanted to visit exotic places but there's no way his old flatbed truck could navigate the world's oceans. He told us once he had read something about some of Amsterdam's special attractions and so that's on his list of places he'd like to visit but never will.

"Wonder how much weight they'd save if they insisted the passengers do the other business?" Perley wondered. "They could offer every passenger a free enema."

"Tom wouldn't need that," I said. "If he ever got close enough to board an airplane."

"This whole thing doesn't make any sense," Purvis said. "First they want you to offload before boarding and then they start selling you beer at 5 bucks a bottle as soon as they get you strapped in."

"I'll bet that's what's behind it," Perley said. "They get you empty before you board so they can sell you more beer and make more money."

Ontari-scary-ario

"I think the sun is setting on Ontario," Big Tim informed me as I settled in for last Wednesday's Manyberries Official Officers Hump Day Cocktail Hour. He was waving some pages he had printed off the internet.

"What, Bob Rae is returning to provincial politics? Garth Turner's joining him to handle all the other portfolios?"

"No, it's even worse than that. The whole province has lost the handles," he said, and handed me the pages.

The first one was about a tractor-trailer driver being ticketed by the Ontario Provincial Police for smoking while behind the wheel of his rig. The fine was $305 for ignoring the Smoke-Free Ontario Act, legislation that forbids smoking in enclosed public and work places. I had already witnessed first hand the zealotry of the nicotine neo-fascists in Ottawa when they slithered into the National Press Club a few times to write a summons for violation of the anti-smoking laws. The Club had a separate room for smokers that, at great expense, had been walled off and ventilated but that didn't matter to the interpreters of the law.

"This guy owns the truck and is the only operator," Tim said. "His cab is his home and office when he's on the road. Yet the cops, backed by some stunted bureaucrats, said it's a work place and has to be smoke free. If there's anything killing industry in Ontario, it's Ontario."

One of the stunted bureaucrats was quoted as saying this application of the law means there's one less place to smoke and it might force people to quit. A representative of the OPP said when a cigarette is being lit you've got fire inside the vehicle. It probably didn't occur to the police that a dashboard cigarette lighter isn't exactly a flame thrower.

"But that's not all," Tim said, and he was obviously on a roll. "Somebody called the Toronto Board of Education claiming that *To Kill a Mockingbird* is a racist book and should be removed from all school libraries. He said it was because the book had the N-word in it."

"As I recall, it uses the word more than once," I said. "Wonder if the author is still alive? She'd no doubt have something to say to anybody accusing her of racism."

"But it gets worse," Tim said, returning to his main thesis. "Somebody in some other school jurisdiction complained that *The Merchant of Venice* is anti-Semitic and puts Jews in a bad light. So whoever the hell was in charge there immediately pulled the books off the shelves."

Tim thanked Hazel for tearing herself away from the final minutes of The Young and the Restless to accommodate our neediness. She asked if we'd heard that the City of Toronto was going to start charging seniors for strolling in groups in a city park.

"Apparently the walkers are paying somebody something to lead their walks and that makes it a commercial venture, so Toronto wants its fair share."

"Now there's an idea for Manyberries," Perley said. "We organize everybody who qualifies as a senior and invite them to walk in the park and charge them for doing it. I bet in a year or two we could get the stop sign replaced. Or maybe even just get the bullet holes plugged."

"We don't have a park," Four-eyed Tom said. "And there's no place we could build one, unless we use Hazel's parking lot on the south side."

"We've got enough people who call themselves seniors, though," Purvis said. "Not me, because I think 'senior' makes it sound like you're old. My wife might join it. She's old enough."

"But remember that guy in Toronto who wants a bylaw to guarantee that there are enough shade trees for everybody who might visit any one of their parks. That would be a big expense if we tried it here – planting trees and then replacing them every spring – because there's not enough rain for them." Big Tim went to university and got two degrees so he's the sort of guy you can rely on for a scientific overview of projects.

"If we used Hazel's parking lot, they could use the smoking benches out front so we wouldn't have to spend any money buying those," Tom said. "And we wouldn't need to buy swings and teeter-totters because old people don't use them."

"Would you guys call yourselves fairly representative of the population of Manyberries?" Hazel asked, and we all nodded yes.

"Then it won't work and I think you should give up on using Toronto as a role model or, worse, a place to emulate."

"Well, it's true that we don't call in the army whenever it rains, snows or the wind blows," I said, "but they must have something there that we'd like to have out here."

"We've got everything Toronto has except for one thing," Hazel told us. "You guys, for instance, come here every day and not one of you walks, even if your various trucks, cars or whatever aren't running, because you call each other to get a lift. If you won't walk the 500, 600 and 700 yards from your homes to here, how in hell do you expect to draw a crowd of walkers?"

"My trailer is more like 900 yards from here," Tom said. "That's more than half a mile."

"Maybe we could talk the old folks into walking a few hundred feet after they get here," Purvis said. "They could circle the parking lot once and then rest on the benches and then come in here for a few drinks before they drive home."

"But then we'd have to get a city council to pass a law saying seniors who walk around the parking lot have to pay a fee. That would mean politicians, living within a few hundred yards of your house. What if our city councillors, if we had any, turned out to be like the ones they have in Toronto or, God forbid, Calgary?" Perley shuddered at the mere thought of it and took a long gulp to settle his nerves.

"Never thought about that," Purvis said, and turned to me. "Write that down as a bad idea so that we'll remember that I had one once."

"What about that time you tried to talk Ottawa into giving religious charity status to ranches?" Four-eyed Tom asked.

Jellyroll Harper

The entire population of the Manyberries Official Officers Cocktail Hour was still agog on Monday when we gathered to debrief on what had happened since we last convened on Saturday. And something very big had happened.

Prime Minister Stephen Harper had gone on a stage in Ottawa and played a piano and sung in front of a room full of people. And he had done it on a Saturday night when there might possibly have been a hockey game on television which he could have watched at a Tim Horton's outlet. Instead he graciously and generously shared his talents with an elite gathering of people nobody in Manyberries had ever heard of. He chose a Beatles tune and was accompanied by Yo Yo Ma.

"Lady and gentlemen," I said, "henceforth our Prime Minister will be known as Jellyroll Harper." I then had to explain to all but Hazel and Big Tim Little that Jelly Roll was the assumed name of a certain Mr. Ferdinand Joseph La Menthe-Morton, one of the finest ragtime and jazz pianists the world has ever known, who launched his career at the pianos of some of the most elegant whorehouses in New Orleans.

The venue where our Prime Minister made his show-biz debut is also fairly elegant. They call it the National Arts Centre and there's no denying that some people from other parts of the nation who have strolled by it while visiting Ottawa paid for it with their taxes, which, as far as some are concerned, makes it national.

"Seems to me," Big Tim said, "that it would have been more appropriate if your Jellyroll had played the piano in the House of Commons in keeping with the tradition of the original's early career."

"Why didn't he do an Ian Tyson song?" Four-eyed Tom wondered.

"You know, we should get a piano in here," Purvis mused. "So that the next time Stephen comes here in an election campaign we could invite him to spend the night playing the piano."

"You're not going to put a piano that big in here,' Hazel said. "That thing he was playing was as big as a wading pool. There'd be no room for customers."

"We could get one of those skinny old uprights," Perley said. "One of those would easily fit between the doors to the bulls and heifers rooms."

"We're going to have to raise money for a landing strip," I said. "There's no way they could land a plane that big in somebody's pasture."

"You're looking at the little picture again," Purvis said. "First we get the piano, the rest is just details."

"If we can't get a piano maybe we could borrow the old pump organ from the church nobody attends," Tim suggested. "He could probably get one of his aides to work the foot pedals."

"What if he calls the election during hunting season?" Perley asked. "There'd be no rooms upstairs for him and all those people he travels with, not to forget all the media people."

"There are enough trailers, fifth wheels and tents around here for them," Four-eyed Tom told him. "I could fix up the canvas on my tent trailer with duct tape and it'd be almost as good as new."

"If we knew in advance that he was coming we could put up posters," Purvis said. "Why, I'd bet money we'd get people coming in from Orion and Etzikom just to say they'd been here."

"Would we headline him as Jellyroll Stephen Harper or Jellyroll Prime Minister Stephen Harper?" I asked. "The cognoscenti will know who Jellyroll was but I'm not so sure that people from Seven Persons will."

"They'll come if you explain what jellyroll meant when Morton gave himself that name," Tim said. "In fact if you put that on the poster, we'll probably get a crowd down from Medicine Hat."

Four-eyed Tom said that he had enjoyed some jelly roll he'd purchased in a bakery up in Calgary. I thought he was going to plug his ears when I explained to Purvis and Perley, in the presence of Hazel, who obviously needed no explanation, that jellyroll was a euphemism for sex.

Perley said that using that headline would be misinterpreted by his political opponents and the media. Hazel saw his point and suggested, based on her own personal opinion, the headline should read the Incredibly Sexy Jellyroll Stephen Harper.

Well, as it happens more often than not, the wonderful, stupendous and boffo idea of an election campaign night musical starring Prime

Minister Jellyroll Stephen Harper in The Just One More Saloon came to naught. That outcome could be easily reversed, however, if Jellyroll agrees to play and sing music and songs more acceptable to Manyberries than that new age and newfangled Beatles music that he performed in Ottawa.

In What Furnace
Was Thy Brain?

It was ordained on a Sunday in what passes for a conference call in Manyberries that the Monday agenda of the Manyberries Official Officers Sports Habitués cocktail hour would be devoted to Tiger Woods. In Manyberries, when the telephone lines aren't in blowdown state, the members are permitted to reserve a topic on Sunday for the Monday agenda. A member wishing to call dibs on first topic has to call all members to argue his case. If he gets no objections, he has to call them all back to say there were none. In the olden days, before e-mail and texting, this was how people communicated. It is probably frightening to some in today's world because it requires a modicum of human contact, even if just by voice.

This time it was Purvis who called to claim first topic and that it would be Tiger. He had read that Mr. Woods had admitted to infidelity, after what seemed like an eternity of media coverage about allegations, that he had indeed jumped the rails of the marital corral and galloped away on more than one occasion.

Purvis said he had looked up the definition of infidelity and while doing so had come across the word "infidel" and that reminded him of a movie he had on VHS: Lawrence of Arabia. He was certain that somewhere in that movie somebody called somebody else an infidel and that it meant somebody who doesn't ride camels. He was going to spend Sunday afternoon watching the movie again. If the word wasn't used in that movie, he also had one starring Errol Flynn and, as far as he could remember, it was about camels and deserts and foreign legions and some guy named Gunga Din.

Big Tim Little and I had made a pact that we were not going to

All Roads Lead to Manyberries

read, watch, listen to or discuss any stories about Tiger Woods. That pledge was made the day the story broke because we both knew that whole forests, tonnes of carbon dioxide and megawatts of electricity would be wasted before we heard the end of it. But as members in good standing, and wanting to remain that way, we had to abide by the bylaws. We had decided early on when the Bald Prairie Rattlers Hunting and Fishing Association was forming that without bylaws, rules and procedures, strict adherence to protocol, respect for those with opposing views and civilized discourse, we would wind up in a shambles not unlike Canada's Parliament.

Tim and I had been as scrupulous in our Tiger Woods non-discussion agreement as we've ever been about anything but it proved impossible to abide by our pact. Tim said he had been listening to a Montana radio station and they played a Hank Williams song, *Your Cheating Heart,* and the disc jockey came on after and said the song was dedicated to Tiger Woods. I said I was reading some poetry and came across a poem by William Blake titled *The Tiger* and wondered if it was some sort of omen.

On Monday we arrived two hours before the official start time of 5:00 to fortify ourselves, only to find that Purvis had arrived even earlier. He had made copious notes he wanted to study and was poring over them while keeping Hazel busy pouring for him.

"I didn't see the whole movie about Lawrence of Arabia because I fell asleep but in the parts I did watch, nobody called anybody else an infidel," he told us. "Same with the Errol Flynn movie but all I saw in that one was horses. There could have been some elephants too but, if there were, I missed them."

We all thanked Hazel for her generosity as she laid down the necessities of life because in the desert-like region in which we live, liquids are essential to survival and life as we know it. The Just One More is the only oasis for too many miles.

"Anyway, near as I can figure, infidel has something to do with religion and not necessarily camels, unless the Arabs have another dictionary. But I've got an idea that could make us a helluva lotta money." He passed me a sketch he had made of what appeared to be a man wearing a head cover with cloth hanging down over the back of the neck. I looked at it and concluded if Purvis ever decides to become a sketch artist, he'll have to go to some school where they teach the rudiments.

"See, this guy Lawrence wore this headgear with this cloth hanging down over his neck, all the way down to his shoulders so his neck wouldn't get sunburned. I'm thinking we get somebody who can sew to make a whole herd of these things. Guys could wear them under their cowboy hats or John Deere caps and they wouldn't have to worry about getting sunburned necks. Hell, it's just as sunny here as it is over there in the desert."

"You're right, Purvis, that is a hell of an idea," Tim said, "I wore one under my hard hat when I was in the Emirates. It beat the hell out of greasy sunblock that sweats off in no time flat."

"I wouldn't bet too many cowboys around here, or anywhere for that matter, are going to wear one of those under their hats or even their caps," Perley said. "They'd probably think they were for sissies."

"Got that figured," Purvis said. "We'll all wear them every day and after a while it'll catch on as a, like a fashion thing, like you know when some movie star wears something and pretty soon all the women are wearing it."

"You know," I mused, "if you turned it around, it'd be a face mask, sort of like the bad guys in the movies wore when they held up a stagecoach or bank, so there's a possible market there too. You'd just have to add eyeholes."

Purvis frowned and pondered that for a few seconds. "Maybe it's not a good idea after all," he said. "We could be accused of adding and betting on bad guys."

"No, there's still hope here," Tim said. "I bet next time he goes out in public Tiger will be wearing something just like that and he *will* have it reversed. Remember those bizarre things Michael Jackson used to wear?"

"How will that help us sell the things?" Purvis asked.

"We just target all the sanctimonious media slugs, pulpit pounders, commentators and tsk tskers who are beating on Tiger Woods and who also committed adultery and you'll have sales in the millions."

"And everybody else out here who hates being called a redneck," Four-eyed Tom added. "Provided they wear it the right way like Lawrence did."

Cowboys and Olympians

It was Purvis who asked if I was going to Vancouver for the 2010 Winter Olympics. Up until just before the end of January this had not been on the radar of the Manyberries Official Officers Olympic Debating Society. It is very likely everybody else in Manyberries had been discussing the Winter Games, but at The Just One More our focus had been on the Ottawa Games, which had been cancelled due to prorogation. As do other great sports venues, Canada's Parliament has its own strict code of conduct, rules and regulations, and proroguing is probably explained fully in chapter 3, subparagraph 4 in a book somewhere. It no doubt clearly states that when the captain of the winning side decides his team needs a timeout he must at least make a phone call to the head referee, also called the Governor General, to inform her of his decision.

It is not a decision taken or made lightly because the consequences have such a profound impact on the health of the Parliamentary Press Gallery. Without the daily Question Period inoculum, members of the PPG are overwhelmed by a scourge known to Greek physicians in ancient times as thanatomimesis.

"I'll have to give that some thought," I told Purvis. "No, I'm not going to Vancouver for the Olympics."

I had to explain that it wasn't a personal boycott but wariness that would keep me away from the Games. This arose from an earlier discussion about rules of behaviour handed down by the Communist bosses in China for the people over there who aren't bosses. They were informed that cursing and spitting were verboten. In all I read or heard about the Vancouver Olympics there had been no etiquette guidelines like that laid down by the organizers. I don't know anybody who'd be comfortable sitting beside somebody who is constantly swearing and spitting. Unless you are the guy married to one of the Manyberries women who drop by here sometimes and whose name I won't mention.

The other, more trivial, reason was that I couldn't afford a standing room only ticket even if I could *get* to Vancouver.

Hazel allowed us to declare The Just One More the Manyberries Official Officers Olympic Venue because she was planning to turn the television over to Games coverage anyway.

We were into day four, possibly five, when Big Tim brought in a story he'd taken off the internet written by some Englishman that some newspaper sent all the way from England to cover the Olympics. After he had passed it around and we'd all read it, a wave of shock, revulsion, loathing, disgust and eyebrow-raising swept tsunami-like around our table.

This English guy had written these would be the worst ever Olympics or something close to that. The details are very sketchy because it was very late when Tim remembered he had stuffed the printout in his pocket that morning.

Tim said it aggrieved him because it came from England, where the last big thing they did on a grand national scale was the Battle of Britain.

Purvis said something about the English being the cruellest race on the planet and pointed at Old Rutherford who had been yanked away from his parents as a child and sent off to the colony to work as an indentured servant through the Child Migrant Program. The only good thing about that terrible cruelty was that we gained one hundred thousand good citizens, Purvis said. He added that you shouldn't be surprised by anything mean-spirited coming from a Brit whose country would do such a thing.

I felt it necessary to offer a defence of English journalists by explaining that they probably came expecting to find cases of free gin and scotch courtesy of VANOC and were no doubt bitterly disappointed.

Perley attributed it to culture shock. He said coming to a city where all the people you encounter have chins and their own teeth would set anybody back.

"The next column this guy writes will no doubt focus on the extravagance of Vancouver hotels," I said. "He'll tell his readers they have bathrooms with soap in every hotel room. And, considering the British Observance in August is an annual event, he'll take home enough soap, shampoo and conditioner to last him for years."

Perley shot back that being yanked out of his own milieu must have made the columnist cranky. "He probably misses the sights, sounds and smells of London. He'd feel like a foreigner in a country where they don't throw their household sewage out the front door every morning and there are no restaurants where the cook boils everything on the plate."

Four-eyed Tom chalked it up to Olympics-envy and went back to his crossword.

Hazel said she disagreed with Tom. "The Englishmen have suffered that *other* type of envy for centuries," she said, "so I don't think the Olympics would make them feel any more short-changed than they already are."

"In addition to world class sports, the Games have a large cultural element," Tim said. "It would be difficult for a Brit to grasp and appreciate that. They haven't had anything cultural to share with the world since Petula Clark appeared on the Ed Sullivan Show."

"But you forget Eddie the Eagle," I said. "The guy came over as a ski jumper in the 88 Games from a country where the landscape is as flat as all the women, except for that Nigella Bites, who does a television cooking show. I think seeing Eddie the Eagle let the world observe a representation of the typical Brit, although I read he might have had a few nips and tucks since then."

"Her name isn't Bites," Tom said, "it's Lawson."

"That reminds me," Hazel said, "the Brits can boast one world record. A few weeks ago, some Romanian woman who weighed 528 pounds gave birth to a 6 pound daughter. But she wasn't even close to the woman in England who weighed 560 pounds and gave birth to triplets."

"Lots of mothers have triplets," Tom said, "even quadruplets, so they can't brag about that."

"I think it was William Makepeace Thackeray who delivered the best thumbnail sketch of the British psyche," I told my confreres. "I paraphrase because it was years ago in Vanity Fair but it was something like *the English reject, resent, ridicule and hate any other race that lives at a level equal to or above English pretensions.*"

"Or who didn't have a need to invent codpieces," Hazel added.

Conlogue

The Prairie

It is a place where you can get just as lost as you can in a forest. Those who love it have lived it and those who haven't lived it will never know what it is to love it. Some will visit and feel larger than life because you cast a longer shadow than anything within sight. There was a time when the bison, grizzly bear, elk, the red deer, antelope and Indians on horseback cast longer shadows but nobody living today remembers that time. Those who love the prairie don't feel larger than life no matter how long their shadow and that is why they love it. What's left of the prairie is still huge, and a lone human is no more than a speck in God's eye.

There are still some spots, my favourites, where you can sling your rifle over your shoulder and within minutes from the truck be as alone and small and quiet as if you were *all* alone, the only human on the whole planet.

There are places where you can find a dip in the land, stretch out and see nothing but blue sky above and hear nothing but the always-present wind rustling the grass. The prairie here still has memories of when it was a vast and empty space, so vast that, possibly, nobody ever touched this small space you are now occupying. If somebody ever did hunker down here, that individual heard what you are hearing today – nothing. No traffic noise, no human voices and, if you can silence them, no voices from inside. Think hard on that – it could be that you and you alone are the first human to ever occupy these two or three square feet of space. If you choose to believe that somebody did stretch out in this shallow prairie depression, allow yourself to imagine that it was for the same reason: to get down out of the wind and rest, or to avoid being seen.

This is good for the soul, if your philosophy accepts such. This is

All Roads Lead to Manyberries

getting as close as you'll ever get to aloneness, not loneliness, but aloneness. It might be the only time in your life you'll ever find the comfort of being completely and utterly alone.

There are some people who can't comfortably contemplate being alone. They turn on television, radio or stereo when alone at home to avoid the silence. There are a lot of people who, rather than go home to silence, will stop off someplace where they can be surrounded by noise, even the voices of strangers. Chances are pretty good the prairies won't have much appeal for them. Some people need noise as a constant in their lives; some of us don't.

Some years ago Harry Charles and I were hunting non-trophy antelope and on the way back to the Suburban we sat down in a depression on a slope to rest, share a chocolate bar and drink some water. We hadn't spoken a word; didn't need to because when one of us hunkered down, the other just naturally did the same. You don't want to interrupt the quiet.

We had been stretched out for a half hour when Harry Charles nudged me and raised a finger and pointed east. He had seen a very large pronghorn, and I mean *very* large. It was curious and over the next half hour circled around and drew ever closer. Finally, it was standing about 40 feet away, watching us intently trying to determine what these lumps were on his prairie. It would have made the record books and made our own two trophies that we got years later look like adolescents, and both *those* were impressive. He stared at us for a long time and then wandered away. We let him get out of sight and then walked back to the Suburban and on to Manyberries. We hadn't spoken by then for nearly three hours and still didn't speak until we were in the Just One More and had our sip of black rum.

"That was something, wasn't it?" I wasn't really asking him for his opinion and didn't have to say what the something had been.

"Yeah, but did you notice," Harry Charles said, "how quiet it was? Even at forty feet when he moved away, all you could hear was the wind rustling the grass."

Ron Wood has been a member of the Parliamentary Press Gallery; television anchorman; federal communications bureaucrat; News Director for CKXL and CHFM Radio in Calgary (winning several regional and national radio awards, including the prestigious National Radio Award for Best Opinion/Commentary Broadcaster); Press Secretary to Preston Manning, Leader of the Reform Party; and EA/Communications Advisor to Opposition Leader John Reynolds. He also handled special communications assignments for Stephen Harper when Mr. Harper was Leader of the Opposition.